Some of the FUNNIEST THINGS *Happen in* COLLEGE SETTINGS

MY JOURNEY

Leo Mcgee

ISBN 978-1-64559-037-8 (Paperback)
ISBN 978-1-64559-038-5 (Digital)

Covenant Books, Inc.
11661 Hwy 707
Murrells Inlet, SC 29576
www.covenantbooks.com

This book is dedicated to the Tennessee Technological University faculty. They kindly egged me on as I attempted, for many years, to humor them each fall at the opening faculty meeting. Their kindness will never be obliterated.

Thanks, dear colleagues! You are the real reason these vignettes are in print!

CONTENTS

PREFACE

Many of us in higher education consider our campuses to be the heart of the universe. Some see the mission of these monuments of bricks and mortar to be more than for teaching, learning, leading, managing, academic inquiry, community service, and athletic entertainment. They are also places for laughter, for fun and excitement, for expansion of social horizons, for establishment of lifetime friends, and maybe even for establishment of lifetime enemies!

While college personnel are stoically engaged in their daily routines, a few of us are able to see the humor in some of our actions. Some are worthy of being forgotten. Others are worthy of being retold. Included herein is a potpourri of vignettes of wit and wisdom. Whenever appropriate, names of characters have been changed. The idea here is to allow the fainthearted to exist incognito.

Acknowledgments

I should like to thank members of my supporting cast in Cookeville, Tennessee, beginning with Laura Clemons, formerly of public affairs at Tennessee Tech, and Wayne Sadler of the human resources office. Laura's interest, enthusiasm, and excitement regarding my attempt at creative writing always energized me. Wayne's keen mind caused me to become more of a critical thinker as we pondered different issues and concepts and ways to express these matters in prose. Then there are others who simply held my hand and offered encouragement. These compatriots are Dr. Heide Marie Weidner, Dr. Earl Hutchison, and Dr. Albert Wilhelm of the English department and Janet Biery, a local English teacher, and Carolyn Brown of the university's honors program. Moreover, I am deeply indebted to Dr. Linda Null for her extraordinary editorial assistance. Colleagues, I am most appreciative of your support and caring attitude.

ME, MYSELF, AND I

I set foot on a college campus for the very first time back in 1959 when I enrolled at Shorter Jr. College in North Little Rock, Arkansas. Shorter is under the auspices of the African American Episcopal Church. Mr. Clement Smith, my principal at T. W. Daniel in Crossett, ushered me there to accept a football scholarship. The congregation at Campground AME Church had given me its blessing.

After two years at Shorter, I crossed the Arkansas River to enter Philander Smith College. At PSC, football competition was more of the same—Negro colleges against Negro colleges.

After graduation, I was off to Chicago to rainbow's end. While a beginning teacher of PE in the inner city during the day, I took my first graduate course at downtown Roosevelt University. This was the first time in my entire life I had been that close to white people for an extended period of time.

Then Ohio State University beckoned me. There, I obtained the master's and PhD degrees. The institution even took a chance on my administrative ability for a few years.

The lure of Tennessee State University in Nashville went directly to my core. The concept of "black brain drain" echoed throughout the higher education arena. In essence, the concept suggested that white colleges were draining black colleges of their best faculty. A few of us were bent on reversing this trend.

My mentor at Ohio State, Dr. Arliss L. Roaden, assumed the presidency at Tennessee Tech in 1974. Three years later, I joined him and remained at the institution for thirty years. Now that I am retired, some events I observed during yesteryears in the academy strike me as being a bit humorous.

WHEN FACE MASKS ON FOOTBALL HELMETS CONSISTED OF A SINGLE BAR

It was 1987. After carefully placing his pipe on the conference table and then getting comfortable in the plush chair, the candidate for the presidency of Mercy State University asked the room full of interviewers, "Do you mind if I smoke?"

Silence.

The senior dean and the most intimidating figure on campus finally responded, "Do you mind if I hold my arm pit in your face for the next hour?"

The senior dean's tenure as dean became history within two weeks after the candidate assumed the presidency.

THE AM&N MASSACRE

I am referencing the powerful Lions of Arkansas AM&N College in Pine Bluff, Arkansas. The college held the distinction of being the only public institution of higher education in the state for Negroes. Realistically, it would have been more proper for its athletic program to compete only with other public Negro powerhouses across the South, the likes of Grambling, Southern A&M, Jackson State, Florida A&M, and Tennessee A&I, not institutions like Philander Smith College.

In the 1960s, Grambling was second only to Notre Dame in sending players to the NFL—the names of defensive linemen Ernie Ladd, Buck Buchanan, Willie Davis, and quarterback James Harris come to mind. Back then, there were no Negro football players in the major white athletic conferences across the South. All of us brothers were playing amongst ourselves.

My institution, Philander Smith College in Little Rock, was among the second-tier athletic programs. It sent players to the pros too—running back, Elijah Pitts of the Green Bay Packers and Geese Ausbie of the Harlem Globetrotters.

Upon transferring from Shorter Jr. College to Philander Smith, I quickly learned that the athletes were not pampered so much at my new institution. As a scared transfer student standing in the registration line, I trembled at the lady behind the desk who asked me in a mean tone, "Young man, what's your major?"

I began to fumble through the cards in my hand so I could hand her my major.

"Young man, what's your major?" she demanded once again.

I now began to look on the floor to see if I had dropped my major since it didn't appear to be among the cards in my hand. Also

I was completely baffled by the laughter coming from the students standing in line behind me.

Now very irritated, the lady said, "Young man, are you a football player?"

"Yes, ma'am," I responded rather meekly.

"Then your major is PE!" she exclaimed. "And don't you ever forget it," she insisted.

During the first week of football practice, I learned very quickly that all of the veteran players dreaded the annual game with Arkansas AM&N College. The game was a long-standing tradition between the two Arkansas colleges. Our home games were held in War Memorial Stadium in Little Rock.

Philander Smith received the ball on the opening kickoff. Benny Johnson from Portsmouth, Ohio, better known as Scat Back, had the ball on the twenty-yard line. To everybody's surprise, he broke several tackles on his way to an eighty-yard touchdown. Our coach and my teammates were ecstatic. Not me, I had paid particular attention to those huge water buffalos during warm-up. Couldn't keep my eyes off them! "There ain't no possible way we're going to beat these corn-fed guys!" I kept repeating to myself.

During AM&N's first series, this huge fullback broke through the line and was headed at full speed straight down the sideline for a sure touchdown. Two players on Philander Smith's team stood between him and the goal line—two defensive backs, Leo McGee and his roommate, Albert James. For some reason, those pumping knees and those long strides looked familiar to me. Looking over the one bar on his helmet, I immediately recognized his face. He was that same guy from Coleman High in Pine Bluff who had, almost single handily, beaten my high school team 62–0. He easily carried 230 pounds on his six-feet-two-inch frame. Albert and I were more like 175 pounds each.

A millisecond later, I concluded that there was excellent potential for me to see my life disappear before my own eyes. There was absolutely no way I was going to tackle that big dude.

I began to take baby steps. Albert James didn't seem to get my drift. Furthermore, Albert prided himself on being a tough little ole guy. His ego was monumental. He and that huge fullback had the most awful collision I had ever witnessed in my entire football career. That fullback didn't even break stride. He galloped on in for the touchdown. The emergency squad rushed Albert James to the hospital. He would never suit up in a football uniform again. His shoulder was crushed in the worse sort of way.

For days, I felt guilty. However, my guilt slowly dissipated when I learned that Albert James had been beating my time with my girlfriend. Now I was delighted that I had taken baby steps.

Early in the second quarter, our team was preparing to punt the ball to AM&N. I had the assignment of making the long pass to the punter. One of those water buffalos across the line from me began licking his chops. To make matters worse, he began taunting me.

"Little ole boy, what you doing up here?" he uttered. "I'm gonna make minced meat outta you."

The problem I now had was I knew that buffalo could possibly deliver on his promise. My knees began to tremble then my arms. That long pass sailed four feet over the punter's head. Coach Douglas snatched me out of the game.

"McGee, what the hell are you doing?" he yelled. "Go sit your chicken-hearted butt down at the end of the bench."

I wanted to thank him. What I really wanted to say to Coach Douglas was "sir, that was awfully kind of you. Your kindness will never be obliterated from my chicken heart."

Coach Douglas really wanted our team to make a good showing because he had played at AM&N and had been the head coach there at some point in his career. At halftime, the score was 48-7.

In the middle of the third quarter, players on our team began to fake injuries. One player, Carl Lee Gilbert, a linebacker, tried his best to avoid making a tackle. That huge fullback was still running rampant. He was literally a one-man wrecking crew. He broke through the line and cut back right and ran smack over Carl Lee. Carl Lee grabbed his arm and ran at a fast pace to the sideline. Coach Douglas wanted to know what was wrong.

Grimacing terribly, Carl Lee said, "Coach, I can't raise my arm no higher than this," raising his elbow about shoulder high. "I think it's broke."

Coach Douglas looked disgusted. He kicked the ground and told Carl Lee to go sit down. A few minutes later, coach yelled, "Come here, Carl Lee!"

Carl Lee took his time coming over to the coach.

"Now show me again, son, how high you can raise your arm?" the coach asked.

"To here, coach," Carl Lee said, again raising his elbow about shoulder high.

"Well, show me how high you were able to raise it before you got it hurt," the coach demanded.

"To here, coach," Carl Lee said, now raising his elbow high above his head.

"Son, get on back in there!" Coach Douglas ordered. "And knock the fire outta somebody!"

Later in the game, Carl Lee came running to the sideline again. His eyes were swollen, nearly shut from the pounding his face had taken.

"Coach, can I come out now," he pleaded. "I see double, coach."

"Son, get on back in there and just hit the first one you see," the coach ordered.

There was a big pileup near our bench.

Coach Douglas yelled out, "Carl Lee, my granddaddy can tackle harder than that!"

"Send the old dude on in!" Carl Lee responded.

The final score was Philander Smith, 7, and AM&N, 72.

SCAVENGER

During my senior year, we got a huge freshman tackle from Detroit by the name of Nathaniel Hooks. I mean huge! He looked like those water buffalos on AM&N's team. He was around six five in height and weighed around two hundred and sixty pounds. He was, by far, the biggest player that had ever claimed a spot on Philander Smith's football team. Frequently, fellow students would find themselves simply standing around gawking at Nate as if he were a circus character. Nate loved it.

From his very first day on campus, Nate became a problem for the coaching staff. He was always hungry. He simply couldn't get enough to eat. The boy was simply in misery all day long because of hunger pains. He began to lose a little weight. His parents couldn't understand why Philander Smith College was starving their baby to death. He would be on the hall phone almost daily nearly in tears, explaining to his parents how hungry he was.

Back then at Philander Smith, there was no such thing as a training table for football players. Nate would beg the girls for their food and would scavenge from the plates of his teammates. That's how he got the nickname Scavenger.

The administration at Philander Smith must have had a binding contract with a company that grew Cornish hens because we had Cornish hens at nearly every meal, breakfast too. Those Cornish hens gave Scavenger a fit. He couldn't understand why the chickens in the South were so small. One night, I was eavesdropping on his conversation with his mother back in Detroit.

"Mama, these chickens down South aren't any bigger than birds," he explained.

Some thirty years later, I had the pleasure of reading an inter-esting culinary research report that focused on Cornish hen. I should like to share my abstract of the report: Although Cornish hen has been on the culinary scene in American for many years, only recently has it reached respectability. It has finally evolved into an American delicacy, according to some of the nation's most eminent chefs. This succulent fowl weighs about one pound and is extremely tasty when well-prepared. There is one caveat, however. This nutritious entrée may lack sufficient density to satisfy the appetite of athletes, espe-cially football players.

Before arriving on the campus of Philander Smith, Scavenger probably had been no further South than the suburbs on the south side of Detroit. He didn't quite know what to make of those farm boys on the team from across the South nor the inner-city slickers from Atlanta, Memphis, Cleveland, and Cincinnati. Little Rock and Philander Smith was a whole new world to him.

As the team was journeying to Dallas on a chartered bus to play Bishop College in the Cotton Bowl Stadium, Scavenger and I shared a seat. As we were sailing along on this long stretch of Texas highway, I couldn't help but notice Scavenger's obvious fascination with those long Texas cotton rows. I was getting dizzy watching them zoom by the window, not Scavenger! He seemed to be mesmerized by them.

Eventually, Scavenger leaned over to me. "McGee, how do they make all of those lines so straight out in those fields?" he asked with great curiosity.

As sincere as I could, I responded to him. I said, "Scavenger, they use a great big ole pencil."

"They do?" he asked.

"Yeah."

"Where do they get a pencil that large?" he continued.

"They have it special made," I said.

"Oh," he said, obviously satisfied.

"Now go to sleep, man."

When we arrived on the campus of Bishop College, they put us up in this really ratty building. It looked like an old army barracks. The bunk beds gave the appearance of being used during the Civil

War. The mattresses were literally about an inch thick. Bugs were everywhere.

Right away, those farm boys began to tease Scavenger about how the chinches were going to eat his northern butt up as soon as the light went off. Somehow Scavenger got relegated to a top bunk. The team trainer was on the bunk below him. After the lights went off, the trainer took one of those huge safety pins and opened it up and, through that thin mattress, proceeded to introduce Scavenger to those southern chinches.

"A chinch just bit me!" Scavenger yelled. "You guys weren't kidding about these chinches."

A minute later, "Oh! Another one just bit me!" Scavenger screamed. "A big one! I'm not sleeping in this damn bed. Those chinches can have it for all I care."

He then jumped off the bunk and spent the rest of the night in a folding chair.

* * * * *

It was now time for the team to head to the stadium for warm-up. As we approached the Cotton Bowl Stadium, my breath was nearly taken away. Cotton Bowl was plastered across the front of the stadium. This was obviously hallowed ground. Indeed, the best of the best teams in the South had trod on this lush soil. I knew because I had seen them at home on our twenty-one-inch, black-and-white TV—Southern Methodist, Rice, University of Texas, Texas A&M, University of Arkansas.

I speculated that the stadium held over sixty thousand. About three hundred fans attended our game. When you breathe really loud, you could hear an echo in the stadium. I had never been on such lush grass. When I fell on the ground, I literally didn't want to get up.

With about thirty-five seconds to go in the game, we were down by fourteen points. Scavenger and I had just made a vicious tackle on this guy. As we were getting off the ground, Scavenger looked up at me with a very serious look on his face.

"McGee, you think we're going to win?" he asked.

"Yeah," I responded. "And on the next play, you better cream the guy with the ball."

"Okay," Scavenger said with this huge smile.

On the very next play, Scavenger was knocked unconscious. The trainer was unsuccessful in his attempt to bring him out of his unconscious state. He was rushed to a Dallas hospital, still unconscious. Since I was the captain of the team, Coach Douglas summoned me to stay at the hospital in Dallas with Scavenger and accompany him to Little Rock when his condition improved.

Around 11:00 p.m. that evening, I heard movement in his bed. Looking groggy and disoriented, Scavenger turned his head to face me.

"McGee, why did they cut the lights off in the stadium?" he asked.

We ended the season with a record something like 9-2. Friends University of Wichita, Kansas, had a similar record. So as a good-will gesture across racial lines, the presidents of the two institutions decided that Philander Smith and Friends University would have their own bowl game.

It was hard for us to get excited about this trip. Most of us were leery about playing a white team. Some were actually fearful. Scavenger thought it was a great idea.

"I played against white players all the time up in Detroit," he bragged. "They're not as tough as you guys down south. I'm going to crack some heads when we get up there! You all will see. I'm going to have a field day on them white boys. Man, I can't wait! Bring it on, baby!"

I only had second-hand knowledge about playing against white players. It was from two of my high school teammates, Isaac Newton and Benny Abson. They had played as freshmen at the University of Nebraska. They said, "Them white boys up at Nebraska were so tough that when they ate an orange, they ate the peel and all."

Toward the end of the first half in our game against Friends, I got hit harder than I had been hit in my life. It appeared that I had run head-on into one of those huge linemen. It felt as if my neck had been pushed down into my shoulders. Then I heard this familiar voice.

"McGee, I'm sorry, man. I thought you were one of them white boys," Scavenger apologetically uttered.

We lost to Friends by the score of 14–7.

* * * * *

The Rockefeller family had a tremendous compound up in the Ozark Mountains in North Arkansas. When they had these big parties, they often hired male students from Philander Smith to work. We always looked forward to going up the mountain to the compound because the wealthy Rockefellers paid well and because some of those expensive spirits made their way to Philander Smith College.

Scavenger obviously misunderstood us and thought that we meant that those spirits were to be consumed on the Rockefeller premises. Halfway through this party of over two hundred guests, Scavenger dropped a tray of food. After the second incident, he was ushered from the banquet hall to one of the cars to go to sleep.

Having had lots of practice, most of us were exceptionally good at balancing two loaded trays of food at once, above our heads mind you. It was a thing of beauty, an art if you please. We could sail through heavy-swinging doors without dropping even a crumb. I got so good at carrying two loaded trays at once that when a strong smell of food reached our campus from a downtown Little Rock hotel, both of my hands would automatically fly up in the air.

By the time the party at the Rockefeller compound was over, Scavenger had made his way back into the building. We were lined up to be paid. Scavenger got in line too. The white guy in charge refused to pay Scavenger.

"You are going to pay me or else—" Scavenger said. Then he seemed to quickly realize what he had said, to whom he had said it, and the geographic location of his current domicile.

"Or else what?" the white gentleman asked rather sternly.

"Or else you're not going to pay me," Scavenger responded.

THE TOILETS DON'T WORK

"Fill her up!" the bus driver yelled through the open door to that puny, diminutive white fellow who looked as if he had been dropped off from another planet, tattered clothes and all. There was no response from that pitiful-looking dude, nothing! A confused expression dominated his grease-smeared face. This puzzled me a bit, but what could I do other than go with the flow? Being puzzled by the behavior of white folks was not new to me. On the other hand, my grandfather was the South's absolute very best at interpreting their behavior. I knew this for a fact. I had observed his skills in this area of analysis for a long time. I had been his protégé for seventeen years, yet I was still lacking to some extent in this regard.

It took that little fellow several hard-earned minutes to figure out how to fit the pump nozzle in the gas tank. It must have been around three o'clock in the morning. That forty-hour trip to Dillard College in New Orleans had gotten the best of me. The ride seemed to have taken forever. We were on our way back to Little Rock. This gas station was out in the middle of nowhere, I mean nowhere! There was not another building or a light in sight. Whether we were in Louisiana, Mississippi, or Arkansas was a mystery to me.

* * * * *

By this time in the season, Scavenger and I had become good buddies—that is, if you asked him. On our away trips, he made a special effort to find out where I was sitting. He seemed to enjoy my company. I suppose he took a liking to the way I tried to school him on the ways of the South.

"McGee, you know every little ole thing about the South, don't you?" he once asked. "You are a heavy dude, man. You know that. Do the other players from the South know as much as you about what's really going on down here?"

"They should," I responded, not really enthusiastic about his line of questioning.

"Man, if I had lived down here all my life, I wouldn't have taken all that stuff from the white folks. I would have kicked some butts."

"Yeah, Scavenger, I know."

"McGee, you seem like a pretty tough guy. Why do you take this stuff from the white folks?"

"It's time to change the subject."

"Sorry, man," he said, looking a bit chagrined.

When Scavenger got up from his seat where we were sitting, I knew right away that there was likely some fun to be had at this hour of the morning, even in the middle of nowhere. You see, my exposé of the ways of the South was still a work in progress. As soon as Scavenger exited the bus, he yelled to the attendant, "Hey, dude, where is the restroom?"

He has already made a mistake!

"The toilets don't work!" that little weasel responded without taking his eyes off the pump nozzle, gasoline flowing into the bus like a flood. Philander Smith College was perhaps making more money for the station owner in one night than was made in a week. Yet the toilets don't work!

Instantaneously, Scavenger became confused. It was all I could do to repress the laughter that was building up inside of me. Those of us from the South had heard that cliché from gas station attendants and merchants all of our lives. It simply meant that restrooms at service stations, department stores, grocery stores, and other places were off-limits to Negroes. Behind the building, behind an oak tree, or tall weeds were acceptable places for Negroes to relieve themselves. Take your pick. Of course, Scavenger was completely oblivious to the areas already reserved, especially for him. Generally on our away trips, the bus driver would find a Trailways or Greyhound Bus Station for us to have food at our own expense and to take care of nature's calls, not this time! This night was different, very different! Perhaps the driver had lost his way, or maybe it had to do with our trek during this time of night.

Scavenger was now in panic mode! He began to turn in circles. I giggled. It appeared that he might be in danger of wetting on himself or even worse! He hightailed it toward the station's opened door. I noticed that the weasel was the only attendant on site. He was standing there at the gas pump, sucking up Philander Smith's meager resources. Scavenger entered the building and approached the sign that read "toilet." He opened the door. A few seconds later, I heard the toilet flush.

"McGee, there ain't nothing wrong with the toilet!" he yelled from the door of the station. I savored the visible relief on Scavenger's face.

That weasel didn't say a word. I could see the fear beginning to engulf him as the bus load of husky Negroes began to parade toward the station.

I had absolutely no idea that using the white man's toilet for the very first time would be so exhilarating! For some unknown reason, it suddenly occurred to me that I might like to return to this venue someday. So for good measures, my territorial mark landed about four feet high on the south wall of this sanctum!

"McGee, why did that dude flat out lie to us?" Scavenger asked earnestly as we were motoring toward Little Rock.

"I don't know," I responded. "Maybe he thought a big mean dude like you might break the toilet."

"McGee, tell me the truth," Scavenger insisted. "That dude thought we were going to mess up his restroom, didn't he?"

"Probably," I answered.

I was not able to sleep during the remaining hours of the trip. I feared that somehow the PSC team would be hunted down during the wee hours of the morning and dragged into jail and severely punished. The team's crime would be breaking southern tradition and helping itself to every last one of the edibles in the station. Scavenger particularly enjoyed the latter. Among many other things he consumed are pork skins, chocolate cupcakes, moon pies. He must have eaten at least ten PayDay candy bars.

Back in Little Rock, I imagined the lashing the weasel had to endure from the station owner:

"Eddie Ray, what the hell-fire happened here last night?" Robert Logan the station owner asked. *"Looks like this place done been to hell and back! What happened in here, boy?"*

"Ah… Ah…" Eddie Ray mumbled while pretending to be working under the hood of a car in one of the two bays.

"Boy, get from under that dat-blame hood and talk to me!" Robert demanded. *"You know you ain't no doggone mechanic! What happened to my place last night?"*

"Them colored boys did it," the weasel managed to say, his throat dry as a bone and on fire.

"You mean some colored fellers tore up my place like this? And you just stood back and let 'em do it?"

"I couldn't do nothing 'bout it, Mr. Logan," Eddie replied, hoping for sympathy.

"What you mean you couldn't do nothing 'bout it?"

"There wuz too many of them. And all of them wuz big ole stocky boys."

"And you just stood back and let 'em have the run of the place?"

"I wuz outside pumping gas in they bus."

"Pumping gas?"

"Yes, suh."

"How many was on the bus?"

"About two hundred."

"Two hundred on one bus?"

"Yes, suh."

"Boy, you crazy as a toad frog. You gonna make me lose my religion. Can't no two hundred people get on one bus."

"They seem like two hundred to me."

"Every dat-blame snack has been cleaned out of the place! Did you collect the money for all that stuff?"

"No, suh. Them boys stole all that stuff while I wuz pumping gas," Eddie responded, again hoping for sympathy.

"I can't believe this. You let some colored fellers wreck my place and steal every snack in here. Where they come from?"

"I don't know."

"Didn't you get a license number?"

"No, suh."

"How did they pay for the gas?"

"In bills."

"Boy, you done cost me a whole lot of money. You fired right now! Now git!"

* * * * *

I gave Scavenger a new name—Moses. He was thrilled!

All Noseguards Should Be Lined Up before a Firing Squad

When I was introduced to tackle football during the lunch hours in seventh grade, the term *noseguard* was not even athletic jargon. Now that I have had years to reflect on it, my junior high chums, no doubt, had a premonition that I had characteristics for such a position which was yet to be discovered. That was not very flattering of my friends. I abhor the thought that way back then, I exhibited even one characteristic of a noseguard, although from the very beginning, I was always one of the first ones to be picked when sides were chosen on the school playground. I was the only one who consistently dared to tackle our biggest classroom peer, Freddie Starling.

Usually I had more blood, dirt, and grass stains on me at the end of the game than anyone else. Frequently I am reminded of the beating my mouth took from the heels of Freddie's shoes during my seventh-grade year. I have a cracked enamel to show for it. But it was all worthwhile. I was revered by my peers, maybe even idolized, and I loved every minute of it.

Once I got into organized football in the ninth grade, the coach convinced me that there was only one gentleman's position in this brutish sport called football. It was center! That's right, center! To me, center was a cool position: (1) The center hiked the ball to the quarterback on every play. (2) After every play, on offense, the center raised his hand so everyone could huddle around him. (3) The center was the first one out of the huddle. (4) There was no defensive lineman in front of the center, giving the center more freedom in blocking assignments. (5) In practice, the center spent most of his time hiking the ball to the quarterback rather than being involved in those humdrum lineman drills. This was a real blessing for me. My football career probably would have been short-lived if I had to go through those repetitive lineman drills. (6) During rainy weather, a towel hung from the center's rump so the quarterback could dry his hands. (7) In many cases, the player occupying the center position was the smallest player on the line. (8) And finally, the most exciting thing about the center position was the center made the long pass to the punter. The center position and I fell in love with each other.

* * * * *

As we began practice during my junior year and my first season at Philander Smith, I realized I had a rather successful athletic career in college. Injury wise, I was unscathed. After our first game, things began to go south for me. I am not sure which one, either Bear Bryant of Alabama, Frank Broyles of Arkansas, or Darrell Royal of Texas had introduced a new defensive position in college football. For sure, it had to be one of them! No one else would have been that devious! The position was called noseguard. We even watched a film which described how the position would fit into the scheme of things.

After watching the film, my heart sank to its lowest level. My whole body began to ache from anticipating the pain all centers would now surely have to endure. Then fear set in because I knew at 175 pounds, I couldn't compete against this new defensive system which was about to be put in place in the football programs across the nation. My career could easily be history. Bear Bryant so much as said that the noseguard position had the potential of transforming the game of football.

The best I could tell, a noseguard had to be the meanest person on the team who would be a never-die, low-life, slop-eating, snag-a-tooth, hog-breath, snotty-nose, wooly-booger Gila monster—a one-man wrecking crew, if you please. Guess where his position was on the line? Directly in front of the center! I wanted to go back to T.

W. Daniel High and slap my high school coach for assuring me that center was a gentleman's position.

As the center on my team, I ran into my first noseguard when we were playing Arkansas AM&N from Pine Bluff. We were also trying to use Darrell Royal's shot-gun system. I had to be carried to the bus after the game. I hadn't realized God had made monsters like that. This wooly booger was so intense that he was foaming at the mouth and grunted like a wild boar on every play. I could see my football career disappearing before my eyes. I didn't think I was prepared for any other position.

The following week in practice, our coach chose Philander Smith's wooly booger. He was Willie Patton from West Memphis, Arkansas, the meanest guy on the team. Coach Douglas went even further. He selected one of the huge guards to practice at the center position, my position! The only position I knew! Now I found myself doing those dumb lineman drills for the first time. My life was falling apart. I wanted to quit the game I had come to love. I couldn't! I had no choice but to stay. No football scholarship, no college degree. I was a total mess. For two games, I didn't play except to make the long pass. No one else was coordinated enough to do this task.

One afternoon at practice, I happened to be close enough to hear the coaches' conversation. It was music to my ears. "McGee is too good of an athlete to be sitting on the bench. Let's try him at defensive back."

Those lineman drills had stripped me of my dignity. This must have been obvious to the coaches. During my first day as a defensive back, God pulled my left hand up from my side and placed my palm in the path of a thrown pass—a one-handed catch, mind you. God then escorted me into the end zone for a touchdown. The rest is history.

I will always hate noseguards! One of my hobbies now is to go to athletic events, specifically to try to identify old beat-up noseguards. Now and again, one crosses my path. Usually I can smell him ten feet away. When I am sure I have made a successful hit, I take a snapshot of him which eventually becomes a target for my basement dartboard. Other photos of them, I take back to my homeplace in Crossett, Arkansas, and tack them on the wall in the old, leaning outhouse just above the two-seater.

SMACKOVER

Smackover was our quarterback and punter. He was an average player just like some others of us at Philander Smith—save one, Elijah Pitts. Pitts went on to become a star running back with the Green Bay Packers.

Smackover was a tall, slender fellow weighing around 155 pounds. He was close to six feet three inches in height but was as slow as cold molasses. On his frequent attempts to run the ball, I never witnessed a play where he ran more than two yards beyond our line of scrimmage. However, this lack of success in forward progress did not dissuade him. He seemed to love broken plays because this gave him yet another opportunity to showcase his running skills. I sensed that his assessment of his athleticism was not in accord with that of his observers. One could easily conclude that he considered himself a gift directly from God.

Despite Smackover's athletic shortcomings, I admired the guy. In many ways, I was in awe of him. So were others. He had the nerves of a "brass monkey!" Even in the AM&N massacres, he never seemed to get rattled. He simply took his punishment like a real man. When the massacre was over, he would be the first on our team to extend a congratulatory hand to the opposing players and coaches. Also he never passed up an opportunity to attempt to boost the ego of his teammates through his wit and humor. This simply endeared him to the troops.

His likeableness transcended the football program. It extended throughout the campus community. The girls simply adored him. He was the best dancer on campus. Athletes and others male students loved to be in his company. Academically, he was an excellent student. And he was well respected by the faculty and administration.

* * * * *

Our quarterback's real name was not Smackover at all. It was the name of his hometown, Smackover, Arkansas. Willie C. Hendrix was his real name. I never knew what the *C* stood for.

Smackover had yet another very significant distinction. He could pass, not the football mind you. He could pass as a white person. He really got a kick out of this. He would occasionally announce to his compatriots that he was going up on High Street to the Walgreen drug store lunch counter for a meal.

"Would you colored boys like for me to bring y'all a milk shake?" he'd jokingly ask before departing.

"White folks, you gonna mess right around here and get yourself killed," came one response.

"Not a chance," Smackover retorted. "I'm too smart. Plus I'm just like them. How they gonna tell me from any of them other peckerwoods?"

On one occasion, a friend and I happened to see Smackover sitting at the lunch counter in Walgreen Drug Store. He simply faced us, discretely thumbed his nose at us. Then he made faces and broke into a huge grin.

I have a vivid memory of my first trip with the team to Dallas. Our first and only stop between Little Rock and Dallas was at the Greyhound Bus Station in Prescott, Arkansas. There were conspicuous signs at the restaurants that read "coloreds-whites."

After we had gotten off the bus, Smackover casually and jokingly made an announcement.

"Sorry, boys, this is where we go our separate ways. I got to go over there with the folks so I can get some of that good food. Catch you colored boys later. Would y'all like for me to bring y'all something?" He released a loud chuckle and departed ways with his compatriots.

Through the glass partition that separated the two groups, we saw Smackover calmly and confidently take a seat at the counter. Moments later, he began his amusement antics—making faces and thumbing his nose at his teammates.

On our side of the partition, we were two to a hamburger while Smackover was eating a full course in the land of luxury.

At season's end during my senior year, our record was less than stellar (1-8). Coach Douglas got the ax. The old gentleman was quite confused about the ordeal. He couldn't understand why the new president would release a person of his stature because of one bad season. After all, he had been a star-running back at Arkansas AM&N and had actually been the head coach there at some point in his career.

"Fellows, it doesn't make any sense," he grumbled at a team meeting. "You give your heart and soul to something that you love more than life itself, and this is how you get treated. This is the kind of young, inexperienced nitwit Philander Smith has as its president. The institution is going to go straight to hell under his leadership."

After Coach Douglas spilled his guts, it was quiet enough in the meeting room to hear a rat walk on cotton. I sensed that Coach Douglas expected us to take some of the blame for his downfall. Not a soul was brave enough to utter a word. The meeting ended.

Feeling guilty, the next day, Smackover and I walked the short distance from campus to Coach Douglas' apartment. Smackover knocked on the door.

"Who is it?" Coach Douglas yelled, noticeably a considerable distant from the door.

"It's Smackover."

"Ain't nobody home," came the response.

"Coach Douglas, I have Leo McGee with me."

"Still ain't nobody home," he yelled even louder.

Administrators Who Decided that Football Should Be a College Sport Must Have Rocks in Their Heads

Nowadays when I enter a football stadium, the first thing I automatically look for is the ambulance. When I see it, I often cringe because I know that there is a good chance that someone will be hauled off for a repair. The cargo will surely have lifetime residual effects from the hospital visit, as I do—broken bones, dislocations, bruises, lacerations, muscle tears, cartilage disruptions, as well as stretched, torn, or severed tendons. Then there are the final stages—severe arthritis, stiffness, immobility, and even amputations. On the other hand, most of us who have trod this path for "academic" acquisition have concluded that the esteem and exhilaration gained from this noble American experience called "football" make it all worthwhile. I am no exception.

One afternoon in practice at Philander Smith, Coach Douglas yelled, "Y'all playing like a bunch of sissies! Y'all ain't hitting worth a damn!" Now looking directly at me, he growled, "McGee, I want to see some blood! It's not a football game unless the opposing team is bleeding like stuck pigs! If y'all practice like this, you're going to play this way on Saturday! And I'm not having any of this sluffing off out here! Now get off your doggone butts and hit somebody!"

A few minutes later, the helmet that belonged to Big Tex, a tackle was at my feet. I considered this to be an opportune time for me to impress the coach. I aimed. And with all the force I could muster, I cracked Big Tex across the nose with my elbow. Blood squirted as if a pig had been stuck!

"That's what I'm talking about, McGee!" Coach shouted.

GETTING UNDER THE PRESIDENT'S SKIN

As far back as I could remember, I had considered myself a pretty good fellow. I was mannerly, a hard worker, and quite considerate of others. Football stunted me academically, however. Over time, Dr. Walter Coker, president of Philander Smith, caused me to call into question the positive concept I had of myself. Dr. Coker was the most impressive person. He really looked presidential—tall, athletic build, proper talker, imposing (very intimidating). Initially he seemed to like me. In due time, however, I got under his skin. What follows is my assessment of my downfall:

Incident number 1. PSC held chapel on Wednesdays at 10:00 a.m. and on Sundays at 4:00 p.m. All students were required to attend. Seats were assigned to ensure that the iron-clad code regarding same was enforced.

Chapel on Sunday provided President Coker an excellent opportunity to show off because he frequently invited a special guest to speak to the student body. He was highly desirous of having a responsible member of the student body to make sure that the auditorium was presentable each Sunday and that the doors to the entrance were unlocked at 3:45. Dr. Coker knew with certainty that there was only one student on campus he could entrust with this honorable task. You guessed it!

Sunday after Sunday during the first semester, I was Johnny on the spot. Toward the end of the second semester, I got a better idea. This was my plan: go over to the auditorium at 3:00 to spiff the place up, leave the doors to the entrance unlocked, go back to my room, and continue napping. After all, seat-checking on Sundays was not nearly as strict as it was on Wednesdays. My new scheme was serving me well!

* * * * *

I thought I was dreaming! The pounding on my door continued to annoy me. Louder, even louder, I was not dreaming!

"McGee!" That seemed to be a familiar voice. "McGee, are you in there?"

Indeed, I recognized the voice. It was Mr. Frank Pogue, dean of students. My heart began racing.

"Yes, sir," I answered groggily.

"President Coker is really upset with you!" he shouted very sternly from the other side of the door.

For what? I thought then scrambled to make myself presentable. I was now standing in the doorway facing Mr. Pogue.

"Never before have I seen the president this upset," Mr. Pogue announced. "I have known him for a long time, even before he became president here, and he has never ever revealed this lever of anger. He said you have embarrassed him in the worse sort of way."

I stood before him with my mouth wide open, my throat dry as it could be.

"You don't know what this is about, do you?" he asked.

"No, sir," I managed to say.

"It's the foyer of the auditorium."

"What about it?" I inquired.

"It's a real mess," he advised frowning.

I couldn't imagine what he was talking about. "What happened?"

"Man, there are leaves everywhere in that place. Obviously, the wind blew the doors open, and every leaf on campus found its way into the foyer. The president wants to see you right now. If I were you, I would hustle over there as fast as I could."

"Yes, sir."

From a distance, I could see Dr. Coker standing at attention outside the auditorium entrance, dark suit and bow tie. His erect posture was clearly revealing his emotions. It was the most dreadful fifty yards I had ever walked.

He lit into me. "McGee, I thought you were far more responsible than this! Just look at this place! It looks just like a pigpen! I have never been this embarrassed in my life. You embarrassed me before one of my most highly-respected guests. He is the president of Hendrix College. You'll hear from me tomorrow!"

He then turned abruptly and went into the auditorium. I was not dressed for chapel, so I took to the Little Rock streets, returning to campus hours later under the cover of nightfall.

To my pleasant surprise, tomorrow never came as Dr. Coker had promised. For sure, he gave me a major demerit.

Incident number 2. Scavenger is to blame! When football season was over, those slick guys from Atlanta, Memphis, Cleveland, and Cincinnati decided to introduce Scavenger and other players to a noncommercial liquid product. It had been hand-delivered by Jim Dandy, a local bootlegger. We were still out on the patio at 2:00 a.m. Suddenly, I found myself staring President Coker in the face. I disappeared. So did others. Not Scavenger, he was too inebriated.

"Young man, do you realize that it's two o'clock in the morning?" the president asked. "It's way past your bedtime."

"Sir, I am not ready to go to bed," Scavenger retorted in his very proper Detroit accent.

"I am the president, and I say it's time for you to go to bed."

"I don't care if you are Coach Douglas. I am not going to bed!" Scavenger retorted this time with more resolve.

A thought must have pricked President Coker's conscious at that moment. *I fired Coach Douglas. He is not even on the payroll. How am I going to get this inebriated young man to bed?* He thought for a minute before coming up with an answer. *That's the dean of students' job! Indeed it is!*

You guessed it! At the behest of Dean Pogue, I was summoned to become Coach Douglas's surrogate!

I could tell that Scavenger's condition had deteriorated quite a bit during my short departure. His language was barely audible.

"McGee, who was that dude that said he was president?" Scavenger asked angrily. "He's definitely not President Lyndon Baines Johnson. I know Johnson when I see him. Does he think I'm stupid?"

"Scavenger, he's the president of Philander Smith," I responded. "He's in charge of the whole campus. Now let's go to bed."

"I'm not ready, man."

"Ready or not, big guy, let's go."

To my pleasant surprise, Dr. Coker never broached this incident in my presence. For sure, he gave me a major demerit!

Incident number 3. The "sit-in" at the lunch counter at Woolworth store in Greensboro, North Carolina, by Negro students in 1960 dramatically influenced the attitude and mood of Negro students on college campuses across the South. Although the lunch counter in the store in Greensboro had been integrated in the spring of 1960, the Walgreen drug store in Little Rock was still practicing its old ways a year later.

Those pretty girls from up north on the Philander Smith campus wouldn't stand for this. When President Coker got wind of the clandestine meetings they were holding, he became irate, beside himself to be exact.

"How dare you people try to get this peaceful campus all riled up," he snorted during his lecture to the student body in the auditorium. "The college has an excellent relationship with the white people in this city. I will not be able to get anyone to contribute another nickel to this place anymore. You think about that. Many of the things we are able to do for you are supported by donors from right here in the city of Little Rock. If any of you students go downtown and get yourselves in trouble, I'll suspend each and every one of you immediately. You can count on it! You will have absolutely no recourse! Your parents didn't send you here to go to battle with the white citizens in Little Rock. Did they? Of course not. This city is still trying to heal itself from the Central High situation."

President Coker preached on and on, his voice elevating, lowering, and cracking periodically. His eyes welled with tears. The beads of sweat on his forehead turned into a gushing stream. His whole face was a mess.

President Coker continued, "I don't want to have to go and defend you and Philander Smith College to those white officials downtown."

He gasped for air. He finally got some, a deep, deep breath of it! There was silence. Now he simply stared at the foolish group of students before him. Seconds later, he turned and stormed toward the door at the back of the stage.

* * * * *

Those pretty girls from up north were more determined to do something about the situation in downtown Little Rock than before, especially Veronica Brady (Cincinnati) and Fran Blackman (Chicago). President Coker's ultimatum kept resonating in my head. *"I'll suspend each and every one of you on the spot!"*

"Leo, we need you football players," Veronica pleaded. "You all should be leading the march. You big ole strong guys can really make a statement!"

"Yeah, we can be blown away first," was the thought that came to mind.

Veronica continued, "Plus, Leo, you are from the South. You should really be fed up with this stuff. Come on, Leo. It's time for you to step up to the plate, man. This is your golden opportunity. You know as I do that good opportunities don't come around very often."

Veronica worked her magic! In the heat of the moment, her charm and my guilt took control of me. I could hear myself breathing. My heart was pounding away as it did during wind sprints in football practice. Minutes later, close to thirty protesters were headed for downtown. There was a handful of football players that led the line—Big Tex, Texarkana, Texas; Lee Townsend, Oberlin, Ohio; Lenel Vaughn, Helena, Arkansas; Harry Smith, West Memphis, Arkansas; Little Tex, Crystal City, Texas; James Wright, Detroit, and Leo McGee, Crossett, Arkansas. When we reached Main Street, several photographers paraded around us every which way.

"Negroes Protest, 2 Arrests, Conduct Downtown March." This story appeared on the front page of the *Arkansas Gazette*, front and center! The faces of those brave souls in the photograph were as lucid as could be. I could only imagine that those of us who appeared in the photo were on the president's hit list. On our way home!

A few days later, as I was walking across campus, out of the clear blue, a female freshman ran up to me. She was nearly out of breath.

"The president said for me to tell you to put your shirttail inside your pants," she said, trying to make her comments as much of a demand as she could.

"What?" I asked, surprised and a bit agitated.

"The president said for me to tell you to put your shirttail inside your pants," she repeated. "He is up in his office looking out the window at you."

I slowly turned and looked in the direction of his upstairs office. Indeed, there was a body poised with his arms folded looking straight down at me. It was as if he was saying, "I'm going to get you if it's the last thing I do."

To my pleasant surprise, Dr. Coker never broached the marching incident in my presence. For sure, he gave me a major demerit!

Incident number 4. At the close of spring semester 1963, I was scheduled for an interview with Mrs. Pogue for a summer job. Mrs. Dorothy Pogue, wife of Mr. Frank Pogue, was the campus postmaster.

"Leo, this is a very responsible job," she advised. "You remember the old saying: 'The mail must get through'?"

"Yes, ma'am," I responded, trying to appear as attentive as I could.

"Well, this holds very true at Philander Smith. What you will have to do is go down to the main post office around six o'clock every morning except Saturday and Sunday and pick up the mail for the college."

"How will I pick up the mail?" I asked.

"On a bicycle," she responded. "It has a huge basket on the handlebars. The college has been picking up the mail this way forever," she said with a smile. "You can ride a bicycle, can't you?" she asked jokingly.

I smiled. "Yes, ma'am."

"All of our mail will be in a huge bag that says Philander Smith College. You will pick up the bag. And the next day, you will exchange the empty bag for the one that's filled. You think you can do that?"

"Yes, ma'am."

"You will also be responsible for delivering the mail to the president's office and other administrative offices. The president likes to get his mail in the morning around nine o'clock, that is when he is in town. If he doesn't get his mail on time, he gets very upset." Obviously, she wasn't aware of my relationship with the president. She continued, "You think you can do all this?"

"Yes, ma'am."

"Okay, you are hired," she said with a big smile, looking relieved that she had found the right person. "Frank says you are a nice young man."

I rather enjoyed my new job. It was fun riding the bicycle every morning, rain or shine. I even learned to ride the bike without holding the handlebars. This was my first time to ever do so. It was so peaceful some mornings. It seemed as if I had Little Rock all to myself. I could literally feel the power of my job when I entered the various offices with a stack of mail. The secretaries were always so friendly. Their anticipation of what was in the stack brought huge smiles. Theirs evoked a smile from me in return. It was as if the mail was the highlight of their day. I felt that I was providing a tremendous service to them and to the college. I felt good inside. I wanted to be a postman for the rest of my life. It occurred to me that I should have majored in postmanship rather than PE.

* * * * *

I received mail from Helena, Arkansas, on a regular basis. Included was a report on James Baldwin's book *Nobody Knows My Name* for my institution class that my girlfriend, Gloria, prepared for me. That French class was sucking the life right out of me. I had time for nothing else.

I made plans to visit Gloria in Helena during the weekend of July 6th and 7th. I was a little skeptical about the trip because the Trailways bus didn't arrive in Little Rock from Helena until 10:30 on Monday morning. To be honest, I was terribly skeptical. But it was the week of the Fourth of July, and I figured some people would be late returning to campus. I would take a chance on President Coker returning late. On the other hand, Mrs. Pogue had made it very clear that he liked to receive his mail around nine o'clock. Gloria and I were longing to see each other. Our relationship was overflowing with love. She was now part of me. She had made my life complete. A visit to Helena was in order. Testosterone has a way of fogging one's mind!

The bus would not arrive in Little Rock until ten thirty. It would likely be around eleven fifteen before I could get the mail to the president's office.

On July 7th, I bid Gloria goodbye and boarded the bus to Little Rock. The taxi didn't seem to be moving fast enough. I was on the edge of the seat. Once on campus, I rushed to the post office. By the look on Mrs. Pogue's face, I knew I was in deep trouble. My throat nearly closed. Then there was pain from dryness. Tears had welled in Mrs. Pogue's eyes. My negligence was obviously hard on her too.

"Mr. Danner picked up the mail," she said sadly, head bowed. "He has already taken it around to the offices. He told me to tell you to come by his office as soon as you got to campus." She then proceeded to put the mail in the boxes, ignoring me.

Mr. Danner was the business manager for the college. I didn't know much about him. He was always in his office, seemingly in deep thought.

"I am here to see Mr. Danner," I said to Mrs. Wilson, the secretary.

"Leo, he's expecting you," she said, forcing a smile.

From the front office, I could see Mr. Danner standing behind his desk. Our eyes met.

"Come on in, McGee!" he yelled, also forcing a smile. He sighed. "McGee, the president is really upset with you," he said, continuing to smile. "He told me to fire you. He doesn't think much of you. He said you are trifling. I tried to take up for you. I told him that that's not what I have been hearing about you. A lot of people on campus think you are a fine young man, one of the finest. The president said it was up to me as to whether or not you got fired. I have the final word. He said whatever my decision was, he would live with it. I also told the president that there is no one else on campus that I would trust to do this job. McGee, you know what?"

"What, sir?" I asked, staring straight through him.

"I'm going to give you another chance."

My throat dilated, allowing me to breathe without pain.

"Where were you anyway?" he asked.

My body now relaxed, I managed a half smile. "I went to Helena to see my girlfriend," I confessed.

"I figured it was something like that because you have been very dependable so far. You are going with that Foreman girl, aren't you?"

"Yes sir."

"She is very attractive and very nice too. You all make a very nice couple."

"Thank you, sir."

"I'm going to give you another chance, McGee. I'll tell the president that I'll personally be responsible for you. I have faith in you, man. I'm kind of putting myself out on the limb for you. I hope you know that."

"Yes, sir, I do. And I really appreciate what you are doing for me."

"I'm glad to do it. I know about that girlfriend thing. I'm counting on you, man."

"Yes, sir. I will not disappoint you."

"I hope not. Because if you do, I'll be in big trouble with the president. You go by and tell Mrs. Pogue that you are still on the job, okay?"

"Yes, sir."

"See you, man."

"Yes, sir. And thanks again."

"Don't mention it. I was glad to do it."

To my pleasant surprise, Dr. Coker never broached the mail incident in my presence. For sure, he gave me a major demerit!

Incident number 5. Mr. Danner wanted me to continue my job in the post office after summer school ended on August 10. The only problem was I had to find myself a room in the city because the dormitories would be closed until September 3rd, the beginning of fall semester. Rufus Bang, an international student from Jamaica, said I could move into the extra room in the house he was renting.

"Rufus, are you sure this will be okay?" I asked, trying to get a definite commitment from him.

"Yah, mon," he responded in his native tongue. Rufus was a member of the track team and had the reputation of being an all-out ladies' man, as well as a con artist. In addition to my desperate need for a place to sleep, I figured I just might learn some new stuff from Mr. Bang.

My interaction with Rufus had simply been in passing on campus. We had never had a serious conversation.

"Mon, the room is sitting there vacant right now," Rufus advised reassuringly. "You can move in anytime, mon."

"Rufus, you mean you have a room that is not being used?" I asked.

"Yah, mon. I ain't kidding yah. The room is ready to be claimed right now."

"How much are you going to charge?"

"Fifteen dollars per week, mon. That's the best you gonna find in Little Rock. The only hitch is, you gotta bring you own bed, mon."

"There is no bed in the room?"

"The fella that was staying in it before had his own bed. When he moved out, he took his bed. Mon, you shouldn't have a problem finding a bed. You oughta be able to get the administration to let you borrow a bed from the campus, heh? You a good guy. They like you, heh?"

"When can I move in?"

"Anytime, mon, any ole time. You know the house I live in, don't you? Down on State Street?"

"Yeah, down on State Street?"

"Yeah, mon."

"You mean I can bring a bed down there any time?"

"Sure, mon. You sound as if you don't believe what I say. I'm a mon of my word."

"Is this a deal?" I asked, extending my hand.

"It's a deal, mon," he responded.

I spent most of the afternoon trying to figure out how I was going to get a bed. I started with Mr. Danner. He said he wasn't sure about taking property that belonged to the college to an off-campus location, but he would check with the president. He told me that, in the meantime, I should be looking around campus for an old bed. Later that same day, I got word that President Coker wanted to see me. I had not been near him since early July. I was a bit jittery. His secretary ushered me into his office. To my surprise, there was a broad smile on his face.

"McGee, I understand from Mr. Danner that you have found a place to stay until school starts in the fall," he said, smiling genuinely. "Is that true?"

"Yes, sir."

"That's excellent. I am delighted about that. Mr. Danner tells me that you are continuing to be a superior worker. He said he has been extremely pleased with your job performance. Did you turn over a new leaf?" he asked, smiling even broader.

"Yes, sir," I said, knowing this was the answer he wanted to hear.

"I am very glad to hear this. You are welcome to take one of the twin beds from the guesthouse. They are not being used right now. Both have practically new mattresses on them. You'll just have to be sure that you take real good care of it and get it back by the beginning of fall semester. You think you can take good care of it and not let it get damaged?"

"Yes, sir."

"Well, you are welcome to use it. I guess you'll want to take the college's truck and deliver it, huh?"

"Yes, sir."

"You can get the keys for the truck and the guesthouse from Mr. Danner. When do you plan to move the bed?"

"This afternoon," I responded, now relieved that I not only had a place to stay but obviously an exciting one. Thanks to Rufus Bang!

"By the way, where are you moving?" President Coker asked.

"I'm moving down on State Street," I confidently responded. I'm moving in with Rufus Bang."

That smile on Dr. Coker's face disappeared instantly. "Rufus Bang?" he asked.

Puzzled, I responded, "Yes, sir."

"I don't know about that," he said, appearing to have second thoughts about his approval. "I don't know whether I can trust my bed to be in the same house with Rufus Bang. Rufus has a very bad reputation. Are you aware of that?"

"No, sir," I lied. "I get along well with Rufus Bang."

"Maybe you do on a personal level, but he has caused the college lots of problems. It has been one thing after another. He almost got expelled from the institution for allegedly beating up one of our female students. Of course, you wouldn't know about that. I just don't know about Rufus Bang. Are your sure you can trust him?"

"Yes, sir," I lied again. The sum of what I had observed and heard about Rufus was that he was a big-time ladies' man.

"Well, I sure don't but if you insist."

I backed the truck into the driveway. George Tuggle, a perpetual Philander Smith student from Memphis, came out of the front door, looking puzzled.

"McGee, what are you up to?" he asked.

"I am bringing a bed," I responded. "Rufus Bang said I could move into a room here until the fall semester begins."

Tuggle looked more perplexed. "Man, you can't move in here!" he advised. "That room has already been promised to somebody else. Rufus Bang ain't in charge of this house, I am. The lease is in my name. Rufus is always going around and promising people stuff. Man, you can't ever believe anything Rufus Bang says. He is just a lot of mouth. He's always trying to act like he's important. A big shot. He ain't nothing. Rufus had absolutely no business promising you a room. I'm sorry, man."

I had been had, big time! Rufus Bang was nowhere to be seen. President Coker was right on target about Rufus. *How can I explain this to him after his warning and generosity? How stupid of me!*

I couldn't face Dr. Coker. I was sure I could not endure a dressing down from him. For sure, he would not hesitate to tell me how disappointed he was in me. That would be too much for me. I was sure of that.

I had to think of something before the end of the day! That huge storage room in the basement of the men's dorm came to mind. The bed from the guesthouse came to rest there.

I got word that there was a room for rent on Chester, near 9th Avenue. I inquired and was granted permission to rent it on the spot. It provided a bed but not linens. Within a day or two, I became comfortable there.

I turned a corner near the student union and came face to face with President Coker. He was still smiling.

"McGee, how are you working out with my bed and with Rufus Bang?" he asked, catching me by great surprise. I had been successful in avoiding him for over two weeks and was hoping that I wouldn't see him until the beginning of fall semester. No such luck!

My head dropped automatically. He waited patiently.

"Dr. Coker, you were right about Rufus Bang," I responded, hoping to evoke sympathy. His eyes were peering straight through me. "He lied about being in charge of the house where he stays. He is not in charge of it, George Tuggle is. And Tuggle said he has promised the room to somebody else."

"See, I told you. You couldn't trust Rufus Bang. Didn't I tell you that?"

"Yes, sir," I agreed, wishing that I could run away before he dug deeper.

"Where are you staying?"

"Down on Chester Street near 9th Avenue."

"Did you need a bed over there?" I should have lied but told the truth. "No, sir," I responded.

His eyes widened. "What did you do with my bed?"

"I put it in the basement in the men's dorm." I replied, bracing myself for the worse.

"No, you didn't!" he said, suddenly raising his voice by several octaves. "You mean you put my nice guesthouse bed over there in that filthy basement?"

"Yes, sir," I mumbled.

"I cannot believe this. I lend you one of my nice beds and you stick it over in that nasty basement. And you didn't have the common decency to come and tell me you made a mistake about Rufus Bang. You go get that truck right now and move my bed out of that filthy basement and take it back to the guesthouse, I mean right now! And you better clean it up before you put it back in the guesthouse!"

"Yes, sir."

To my pleasant surprise, in my presence, Dr. Coker never again mentioned my negligence regarding his guesthouse bed. For sure, he gave me a major demerit!

Mr. Danner asked me to continue my job during fall semester since I had six hours to take to complete the requirements for my degree. I was successful in avoiding President Coker even though I took mail to his office on a daily basis. Inevitably, however, he caught up with me. It was in late November, and he sent me on a job interview with a company that was new to the city. But I had Chicago on my mind, not Little Rock. The next time I came in contact with him was on the campus lawn at graduation in May of 1964. There was a great big smile when he shook my hand and handed me my diploma. He wished me well!

As a lowly undergraduate at Philander Smith College, I only got a whiff of the college presidency. Interestingly, however, my interactions with President Coker prodded my curiosity about presidential characteristics.

Some forty years later and through the eyes of a twenty-two-year-old, this is my assessment of Dr. Coker.

- Exhibited an impressive swagger
- Wished football had never been discovered
- Force fed the student body Cornish hen
- Tended to weep and sweat at the same time
- Wore his emotions on his bow tie
- Had an inviting grin
- Possessed a heated heart

LEVITY IN THE TOWER

One of my colleagues at Tennessee Tech proceeded to check his voice mail. The female caller's message was "sorry, I have the wrong number. Sir, I don't know who you are, but you are really hot."

The professor took a deep breath and smiled, his ego sailing through the roof. He thought, "Where were you thirty years ago?" The professor was in the postretirement program.

WOW! BUCKEYE COUNTRY

In 1967, there were approximately forty-five thousand students on campus, mind you! What was I doing trying to matriculate at Ohio State University? Not sure, but I gave it a whirl—taking seventeen hours in preparation for a teaching certificate at the elementary level. Already in hand, I held a bachelor's degree in health and physical education from Philander Smith College. I had also managed to complete a three-hour graduate course in psychology at Roosevelt University in Chicago.

After a three-year stint as a PE teacher and coach in a gang-infested community in Chicago, I knew it was time to try something different. So I rented a U-Haul and headed east toward Columbus, Ohio, with my wife and three-year-old on my heels in our '65 Volkswagen beetle. At the time, it never occurred to me that I would remain on the OSU campus for a total of six years—completing the master's and PhD degrees and enjoying employment there. Being in this environment was perhaps the most enriching and enjoyable time of my career in the academy.

I had envisioned registration being a "bugger bear." It was not. Finding my classes was, however. As a youngster, I had been able to navigate miles upon miles of dense and not so dense forest during hunting and fishing expeditions back in Arkansas, not so at OSU. The vast open space simply took my breath away. No matter how intensely I attempted to study the campus maps posted at strategic locations, they were beyond my comprehension. After two weeks of trekking back and forth and guessing, I managed to arrive on time at all my classes in five different buildings.

Throughout my study at OSU, there were never more than two or three of my kind in any of my classes. On several occasions, it was just Chuck Reese and I. Chuck had come from a privileged background. As a youngster, he had attended OSU's campus school and had also received his bachelor's degree from the institution. He never passed up an opportunity to exhibit his self-assurance and intelligence.

The two of us were in a master's-level statistics class. The course was a team taught by Kim Choi, a PhD student, and Dr. Andrew Hefner. Professor Hefner informed the class that out of a possible score of 100, the highest score made was 62, and the lowest score was 19. My heart began pounding out of control. I knew for sure who had gotten the 19. I figured I might as well throw in the towel and return to my job as an elementary teacher in the city school system there in Columbus. I was the third person to receive his test paper. I slowly eased my paper between my knees. Aghast, I was sure I had received the wrong paper. There had to be a mistake. Neatly written at the top of my paper was the score, 32.

After handing out all of the papers, Hefner coyly asked, "What did you all think of the test?"

"I thought it stunk!" someone bellowed from the rear of the classroom. Along with others, I turned to identify this "brass monkey." It was Chuck Reese! I slid down as far into my seat as I could.

There was complete silence in the room. Dr. Hefner was crimson from the neck up. Baffled and embarrassed, he managed to speak. "Chuck, you sure don't mince words, do you?"

"Hell no!" Chuck exclaimed. "I believe in telling it just as I see it. I don't think anyone on this campus has ever accused me of sugarcoating anything. There were some very dumb questions on the exam. Who gives a damn about what Choi or Hefner thinks? I want to know what authorities in the field think about certain aspects of statistics, not what the two of you think. In a nutshell, those are my feeling about your sorry exam. Obviously, you are very proud of it. I am not, far from it as a matter of fact."

Silence.

No doubt this was a new experience for Hefner. He managed to open his mouth. For a moment, nothing came out. He spoke ever so slowly and cautiously, "I'm going to write your name."

Chuck cut interrupted. "Not in your damn black book, I hope."
Laughter filled the room. Professor Hefner dismissed the class.

* * * * *

The early 1970s was an era of student unrest. In the eyes of some, these were the heydays for black students on major college campuses. They commandeered buildings, made strict demands, and disrupted major campus operations. These activities weighed heavily upon the minds of university administrators, causing them to problem solve and behave in ways that they were unaccustomed. The "adversaries" also behaved in ways uncommon to themselves as a result of their newly discovered bravery and freedom.

This newly discovered empowerment caused black students to be unmerciful toward the recently hired "Negro expert" in the college of education at OSU. Jasper Kriskovich, from Cleveland, Ohio, had many successful years of experience as a school system administrator in the inner city. His primary responsibility was to develop an urban education emphasis in the college. Black students on campus had their own agenda and were not at all pleased with the one touted by the "Negro expert."

Kriskovich declared that he would not be deterred and meant it. He did not appear to be easily rattled. He was around five feet eleven inches in height, stocky, and street-smart.

From the black students' perspective, a confrontation with Kriskovich was in the making—indeed a necessity. He had refused all invitations to meet with the students. Who was going to "bell the cat?" Chester Martin from Detroit was coaxed into this endeavor. His comrades watched his actions from a distance down the hall.

Banging on Jasper Kriskovich's door, Chester defiantly yelled, "Kriskovich?"

No answer.

"Kriskovich?"

No answer. Chester banged louder. Now exceedingly loud laughter came from his compatriots down the hall.

"Kriskovich, I know you are in there!" Chester announced. "We want to talk to you, man. Stop hiding behind all that theory mess. Come out and talk to us like—" The door to Kriskovich's door suddenly popped open, surprising Chester mightily. He jumped back, nearly falling over backward. A roar of laughter echoed down the hall.

"What the hell do you want?" Kriskovich demanded.

Chester's state of shock rendered him speechless. Sensing that his action had momentarily defanged the aggressor, Kriskovich took a step backward and slammed the door.

When Chester's sensibilities kicked in, he found himself transfixed in front of Kriskovich's door, mouth wide open. He was not quite sure what had happened or what to do next. Now the laughter coming from the other end of the hall was much louder and constant.

Ordinarily when Chester entered the sanctum of the black student lounge at the other end of the hall, he felt a true sense of comfort and belonging. Today he knew for sure that it would be very different. It seemed an eternity for him to walk from Kriskovich's door back to the lounge. Before entering, he made a gallant attempt to brace himself for the worst. He hadn't felt this horrible since he wet in his pants in first grade.

Silence.

Uncontrollable laughter! Signifying!

"Man, I can't believe you let that white dude shake you up like that. You almost broke your neck when that dude opened the door. I thought you were going to take off and run back down here and get up under Karen's dress. How can a tough black dude like you from Detroit freak out like that? Man, you gave that 'Negro expert' more confidence."

During this endless session of signifying, Chester did not utter a sound. Rudolph the Red-Nosed Reindeer entered his mind. No longer would he be able to join the reindeer games. Santa was not there to save him. He was all alone. He would become the joke among blacks on campus. He could not deny that he was intimidated by Kriskovich. His compatriots had witnessed it with their own eyes.

Words of the confrontation between Chester Martin and Jasper Kriskovich quickly got around the college. As a result of this confrontation, Kriskovich experienced a higher-level respect from his colleagues.

"You have got to stand up to them," Kriskovich advised the college's executive council.

The "Negro expert" was never to be challenged again by the black students. He went on to have a brilliant career in higher education as an expert in urban education.

Chester never completed the graduate program at the institution.

MISTAKEN IDENTITY

I simply could not understand why this young man in my graduate class at Tennessee State University was insistent that I come and watch him coach the basketball team at the state prison. Maybe it was because I had perhaps mentioned in class that I had played college football. Who knows? I sure didn't!

Richard Williams was a bit different when compared to other students in class. Nearly all were school teachers in Nashville and surrounding counties who were taking courses for increased salary increments. Richard was an employee at the state prison and was the basketball coach there. I doubt that anyone could have been prouder of his job than Richard. He never passed up an opportunity to reference his job, whether in class discussions or at breaks. He seemed to simply love what he was doing for a living. I sensed that he considered the prison to be the state's most worthy enterprise.

Richard cornered me one night before class began and tried to get me excited about an upcoming game between the prison team and Fisk University.

"Dr. McGee, you have got to see this game," Richard pleaded. "Fisk has a good team, but my team is a lot better. Several of my guys have played college ball, one at a big university. He's good enough to play in the NBA."

"NBA?" I asked.

"Yes sir," he responded. "Dr. McGee, this guy is good. You have got to come out and see him play. He's like a magician, and he can really shoot."

This NBA thing kind of pricked my interest although I wanted no part of going inside a prison. I had known lots of people who had taken up residence at such facilities for varying periods of time, including three of my nephews, various schoolmates, distant cousins, and others. I had vowed never to be caught behind prison walls.

"Dr. McGee, a lot of people have this real bad image about our prison system," Richard continued. "Really and truly, it's not all that bad. I am out there all day. I just try to take the good with the bad. Dr. McGee, you don't have to give me an answer today. The game is two weeks away."

"What's the protocol for visitors getting inside the prison?" I asked.

"It's easy," Richard answered excitedly. "You'll be with me. I'll meet you at the front gate, and I'll have a pass for you. The warden would be impressed by having a professor from TSU on site. You'll really enjoy the game, Dr. McGee. Can I count on you?"

Silence.

"Maybe so," I responded, cautiously. *What am I getting myself into?* Richard went through a list of rules for visitors:

1. Do not wear a tie, this makes you stand out too much.
2. Do not wear jewelry—not even a watch. It's too tempting to the inmates.
3. Do not wear dress pants. Wear khakis instead. This allows you to blend in.
4. Do not wear dress shoes. Wear old sneakers instead. This also allows you to blend in.

"Look as much like a prisoner as you can is what you are telling me, right? Thanks, man."

I met Richard at the front gate of the Tennessee State Prison. He was exceedingly happy to see me. He gleefully introduced me to every guard within hearing distance. He put emphasis on "Dr. McGee, professor from TSU." Who gives a cotton-picking hoot?

We walked through an endless number of doors; and each time one slammed behind us, my trembling knees got weaker. By the time we reached the dingy and dark basketball arena, my knees were so wobbly I could hardly stand. Bleachers were only on one side of the facility and were already filled to capacity with inmates. I felt like a fish out of water.

"Coach, who's that sweet thang you got with you?" someone yelled from the bleachers.

"Keep your eyes straight ahead," Richard whispered sternly. Then he caught me completely by surprise. "You can wait here on the team bench while I go and get the team." His comments were more of an order than a suggestion. In essence, his behavior implied "buddy, you swallowed the hook and sinker!" This surprised me even more. *I knew I should not have put myself in this predicament! Only I am to blame!*

I wanted to plead with Richard to let me go with him, but that would have been too embarrassing. Then I told myself that there must have been some prison rule that prevented me from accompanying him. Surely he knew how frightened I was.

The heckling directed toward the visiting professor by the prisoners was degrading and constant. It seemed to have taken forever for Richard to bring in the team. All the while, I sat ever so quietly and motionless enduring all sorts of suggestive remarks, remarks that I didn't know existed.

As the two teams warmed up, I felt my body relaxing. I tried to pick out the NBA prospect. I was not confident that I could.

Fisk got the tip-off, and the recipient drove the entire floor for a layup. The inmates booed incessantly every time Fisk had control of the ball. Conversely the rowdiness intensified each time their side had possession of the ball. It was pure pandemonium when the team scored.

At the half the score was 45–45. With fifteen seconds to go in the game, the score was Home, 96, Fisk, 95. Fisk was in possession of the ball on the opposite end of the court. When that little guard finally got the ball over the midcourt line, there were five ticks left on the clock. The spectators were pretty much out of control now. With two seconds on the clock, that little fellow eluded the competition and let one fly. The ball went straight through the goal, and the place erupted with boos!

Suddenly I realized I had committed the cardinal sin. I was totally unaware of my exhibition. I was standing there proudly cheering for Fisk. Unforgivable mistake! I felt something hit my head. Then something hit me in the back. When I turned to the stands, I was facing my worst nightmare. Fingers were pointing at me like daggers. The expletives were penetrating my soul. I was horrified. I looked for Richard. He was nowhere to be found. He and the team had disappeared during the melee. There I was standing on the gym floor all alone with hundreds of agitated prisoners. The guards were trying frantically to control the inmates and to usher them back to their cells.

One of guards noticed that I was on the gym floor. He began to seethe even more. "What the hell are you doing down there, dummy?" he growled. "Get your butt up here!"

"I am a guest." I pleaded.

"I know!" he barked. "We all are guests. Now get your butt up here, or do you want me to come down there and whack you over the head with this stick?"

"I am a guest of Richard Williams, the basketball coach. I am a professor at Tennessee State University. Richard invited me to watch the game."

"He's pulling your leg, Bo!" one of the inmates yelled. "He ain't no professor at Tennessee State. He dressed just like we is. How come he gits to stay in the gym, and we don't?"

The guard was now agitated enough to shoot me. Only if he had a gun! "Buddy, you got three seconds to get your butt up here," he ordered. "Don't make me get real nasty with you."

I was petrified. I envisioned being taken to a cell block, never to return alive.

As I stood there, I watched that stocky guard sling his huge black boot over the rail to come and show me that he meant business.

"Bo, he's okay!" another guard yelled from high in the bleachers. "He came in with Richard."

"You sure?"

"Yeah. I was there when Richard checked him in at door three."

Disappointed, the guard climbed back over the rail and went about his business. Like cattle rustlers, the guards cleared the gym within minutes. I exhaled. I questioned my sanity. *What on earth had I done to deserve this? Where is Richard?* Voices of the irate inmates were simply echoes now. I could hear doors slam in the distance. Then there was total silence. I made a gallant attempt to pull myself together. Suddenly the lights in the gym shut off with a muted thump! There was total darkness, except for a small slit of under the stairwell door! I panicked! My intuition guided me to the slit of light. I slowly opened the door and decided to take the stairwell downward. One level below, I faced a steel door that was locked. I banged on it for several minutes. Nothing! I banged again, nothing! Then I thought I heard footsteps. Could it be Bo? The door slowly opened. There stood Richard! I wanted to give him a big hug but constrained myself. Embarrassment was etched in his face.

"Doc, I am so sorry," was all he managed to say. "I forgot all about you."

I gave my first F in a graduate course at TSU!

Thou Shall Tag Along
behind Thy Mentor

All of us who have or have had careers in the academy know the tremendous value of an exceptional mentor. I was told early on that the more mentors one has, the merrier! Throughout the history of higher education, individual careers have been significantly enhanced simply by an affirmative nod from a mentor. The value of such individuals should never be underestimated.

At OSU, I was fortunate enough to have two stalwarts in my camp, Dr. Arliss Roaden and Dr. Luvern Cunningham. Dr. Roaden was dean of the college of education when our paths first crossed. He later became vice president of research and graduate studies. Dr. Cunningham succeeded Dr. Roaden as dean of the college of education.

When I was a doctoral student in the college, Dr. Roaden appointed me to the position of director of clinical experiences. The new director of clinical experiences got a hefty salary plus tuition remission and a prized-A parking sticker, the ultimate of parking stickers. Before the exhilaration subsided, I found keys in my pocket to a brand-new Pontiac Grand Am—air conditioned, power windows, power seats.

"What have I done?" I asked myself. "I can't park this big ole thing in the Arps Hall parking lot! I will likely be run out of town by other doctoral students!"

My new Grand Am never came within a quarter of a mile of Arps Hall.

* * * * *

Once Dr. Roaden became president of Tennessee Tech and I was a department head at Tennessee State, word got to me indirectly on several occasions that Dr. Roaden would like for me to visit his campus. I eventually honored the request. And, while on campus, I got the distinct impression that I should apply for an assistant dean's position there. I mentioned this to my wife, Gloria.

"Cookeville?" she asked with an expression of disbelief. Nashville was supposed to be our last move. "Where is Cookeville anyway?"

"East of Nashville, about eighty miles," I mumbled, hoping to calm her.

"I thought Nashville was going to be our last move."

"I did too, but Dr. Roaden is my mentor. He opened doors for me at Ohio State. There is no doubt that he will continue to have a positive influence on my career."

"Cookeville is one of those really small towns, isn't it?"

"Yes, about twenty thousand."

"And you want us to move there?"

"Maybe."

Gloria became very quiet, tears welling in her eyes. I felt terrible. During the twentieth century, Negroes had left the South in flood tide proportion for big cities in the North and West in search of a better way of life. The McGees had also. Now we were pondering a return to small town America.

To put Gloria's anxiety in abeyance, I knew what my next move had to be. I would drive to Cookeville to sniff the place out. That's exactly what I did. My first stop was at a service station. It looked like the ideal place to get accurate information about the city.

"Good morning, sir," I said to one of the attendants. "How are you this morning?"

"I am wonderful," the attendant said with a huge smile on his face. "If I had it any better, I doubt that I could stand it. You are not from around here, are you?"

"No, sir," I responded. *How did you know that?* I wanted to ask him.

"I didn't think so. I know nearly all the colored boys in Cookeville. I knew your face didn't look familiar. You got business in Cookeville?"

"Yes, sir. I am thinking about looking at a job at Tennessee Tech. And I came up from Nashville to see if I could find out something about the town."

"You've come to the right person. I've been in Cookeville all my life. I know most everybody and most everything about this town. If I don't know the answer to any of your questions, I can find the answer in a heartbeat. Now what would you like to know about this great town of ours?"

"Are there many blacks in town?"

"There are a few but not as many as you might think there should be for a town of this size."

"Where do they live?"

"On the west side of town, in a section we called Bushtown."

"Where is Bushtown?"

"Just down the road from here. When you come upon a juke joint on the left, go back in there behind it, and you'll see several houses. Some of the coloreds have real good houses."

"How do the two races get along in Cookeville?"

"Fine and dandy," he responded with an air of pride. "The coloreds and the whites get along just fine in Cookeville, always have. The schools integrated years ago without a hitch. There was not a crossword from anybody. That's the kind of town Cookeville is. The races are almost like family. The old folks on both sides have known each other years, from the time this town was settled I guess. Me and some of them colored boys are the best of friends. We cut up with each other all the time. We hunt and fish together all the time too. Colored people are some of my best customers."

I drove back to Cookeville again and then again. I took Gloria and the girls over one evening as well. This was the quietest trip we had ever taken, bar none. Cookeville it would be.

We arrived in town at the Saxony Apartments complex in January 1977. During our various trips around town, we would look for other blacks. We rarely ever saw any, however. When we did, there was a light celebration in the car.

"There is one!" someone would say with excitement.

"Where?"

"Over there by that church!"

"Sure is! The first one we've seen today."

"There are two more!"

"Where, honey?"

"Over there, sitting in that car!"

"There sure are. Three today."

This became the girls' favorite pastime when we were out journeying around town. There was virtue in being the first to locate a black, as well as to locate the largest number. As we were on Interstate 40 in Nashville one Saturday, Jennifer, our four-year-old, was jumping up and down on the back seat of the car yelling at the top of her voice, "Mommy! Daddy! There is a whole bunch of them!"

"Where?" Gloria asked.

"There!" We could easily see what prompted Jennifer's excitement as a school bus packed with black faces zoomed by.

Little did we know what an impact our dog, Loppy, would have on our relationship with the Cookeville community. Prior to Cookeville, Loppy had inhabited a black community. A few weeks after our arrival in Cookeville, we began to see a side of Loppy that caught us totally by surprise.

Tom Furtsch, our neighbor and a faculty member in the chemistry department at Tech, jogged four to five miles per day. Professor Furtsch became Loppy's favorite target. She would hide behind a shrub in our yard, and within a flash would be yapping inches from Tom's heels. On occasions, I would hear harsh expletives coming from the direction of this esteemed professor.

Just before departing for a two-week vacation during our first summer in Cookeville, I delivered Loppy, on a leash, to a boarding and grooming business. Upon our arrival, she was quite unruly.

"Ah, she'll be all right," the gentleman who owned the business said confidently. "She'll eventually calm down. She's among strangers and is in a strange place as well. She'll be all groomed and pretty when you get back."

I was overjoyed.

When I returned a week later, I didn't see Loppy anywhere in the grooming area. The owner slowly appeared.

"Does you dog act up at home?" he asked, looking puzzled.

"No, not really," I lied, rather meekly.

"Well, I really think your dog is prejudiced," he said. "She wouldn't let anybody touch her. In fact, she acted so bad we had to tie her up out yonder in the barn."

At vacation time the following summer, I took Loppy, on a leash, to another boarding and grooming business. The owner was a rather tough-looking lady. As the summer before, Loppy went through an unruly routine when I delivered her to the groomer.

"Loppy is a little different," I said rather softly.

"We'll get along just fine," the lady said with assurance.

Again, I was overjoyed.

Upon my return, Loppy was prettier than ever. She had been groomed and had a little red bow on her head. The groomer was even carrying her in her arms. My heart skipped a beat.

"How did you all get along?" I asked rather cautiously.

"Oh, we got along just fine once I figured out what her problem was."

"What was her problem?" I asked.

"Loppy is a very prejudiced little dog!" she said with resolve. "It's plain and simple. She doesn't like white people. Not at all! After we had a little heart-to-heart talk, she has been as sweet as apple pie."

INTEGRATION TO CELEBRITY STATUS

Off-campus course offerings are almost as ingrained in Tennessee Tech's history as the engineering program. Because of the institution's distance from major population centers, it is relatively safe to say that its academic off-campus program took the lead among universities in the state in this regard. As a new assistant dean in the division of extended education and associate professor of education, I was expected to go to these remote sites to impart knowledge too. For me, of course, I was to impart to those of a different hue. Nearly 100 percent of these communities were ethnically homogenous. In some cases, they were places where no blacks had ever traversed. My kind was indeed foreign to those parts.

"Leo, it would be good for you to go out there in the hither land," Charlie Golden, a trusted colleague in the division, said. "They need to see and mingle with you, and it would be good for you to do the same." I was struck by Charlie's sincerity. He continued, "These people need to interact with you too, you know. Many of them have never had the opportunity to converse with blacks. They grew up in those communities, came to Tennessee Tech for their degrees, and went back home. You need to go out there. You don't have any appre-hensions about going, do you?"

"Oh no," I lied, not knowing at all what I was getting into.

"I'll get the students and the community prepared for you. Don't worry. You can trust me. They are fine and upstanding people. I think the first place I'll send you is Oneida, Tennessee. Have you ever heard of it?"

"No," I responded, trying to steady my voice.

It's northeast of here, right on the Kentucky line. It's about two and one half hours away. You need to leave in plenty of time so you can find the hotel where you'll be staying. Leo, there are no blacks up there, not one black soul! Does that bother you?"

"No," I utter, my throat constricting. For the first time, my heart began pounding. At that moment, I wished that I had never left Nashville—to heck with a mentor.

Charlie continued, "Leo, your class will meet on Saturdays from 9:00 a.m. to 4:00 p.m. You will need to leave on Friday afternoons and spend the night at Tobes Motel. Leo, no black person has ever stayed at Tobes Motel. But don't you worry about a thing. I have known Jack Tobes for twenty years. He's a prince of a good fellow. He's one of the finest people you'll ever meet. I told him you were coming. He promised me that he would take care of you. When Jack says he's going to do something, it's like money in the bank.

"Jack is pretty well off, so he doesn't have to listen to other people too much. He's very independent. He kind of does what he wants to do." Charlie paused for a moment as if he were gauging my expression. I hadn't said a word. I had simply stood there with my mouth open. "I promise you, Leo, you don't have a thing to worry about."

* * * * *

I walked into the front door of the motel, or so I thought. There was no registration desk! Rather, there was an elderly gentleman slumped on a couch fast asleep in front of television that was relatively loud, nearly blaring. I quickly concluded that I had walked into someone's living room. *Now I was an intruder! A burglar! Get yourself out of here, man! Oneida, please have mercy on me. I beg of you.*

I tried to still myself as much as possible. The instant I began my backward departure in search of the registration location, I heard movement on the couch. The old gentleman sprang up and headed toward me, smiling. The tension soothed my body as it dissipated.

"You must be Dr. McGee?" he asked in a friendly tone.

"Yes, I am," I responded, relaxing even more.

"I am Jack Tobes. Dr. Golden informed me that you were coming. We are delighted to have you in Oneida and at Tobes Motel. Dr. Golden said an awful lot of good things about you. He tells me that you are a pretty good fellow. Was he being truthful?"

"I would like to think so," I replied, thinking that this old dude is okay.

"I want you to know that we are glad to have you at the motel. We are thrilled to help Dr. Golden and Tennessee Tech out in any way we can. Tech is a fine university. We have a lot of youngsters from Oneida who go down to Tech and get degrees."

The living room of the Tobes's home was indeed the registration area.

I could feel Mr. Tobes's eyes penetrating me, but that was okay. I had given him the once over and had concluded that he meant well and perhaps should be applauded for integrating his hotel at the behest of Charles Golden and Tennessee Tech. What a monumental feat!

He cleared his throat and then caught me by total surprise. "We want you to have some supper with us," he said, smiling, exposing pipe-stained teeth. There were several pipes on the coffee table. "You haven't eaten this evening, have you?"

"No, sir," I replied untruthfully. I had stopped at a fast-food joint in Harriman. What the heck.

"Good. Emma Lou has cooked a great supper. She's got blackberry cobbler for dessert. Sounds good?"

"Yes, sir, it sure does," I responded, my mind briefly drifting back to the numerous days of blackberry cobbler in Arkansas.

Mr. Tobes took me through a door right into the dining room. He introduced me to his wife. She directed me to the bathroom to wash my hands. Mr. Tobes followed. We were now seated at the table for supper.

"Dr. McGee, do you have children?" Mrs. Tobes asked.

"Yes, ma'am, I do," I responded. "I have two girls."

"We have two children too, boy and a girl," she offered with a sense of great pride. "They are both married and have their own families. We have five grandchildren." She paused for a moment. "How old are your girls?"

"Eleven and four. The eldest is in the sixth grade, and the youngest is in preschool."

"There are quite a few years between them, aren't there?"

"Yes, ma'am, there are. That has its positive, as well as negative points."

The food was simply delicious, as good as I had ever eaten—corn on the cob, cabbage, fried okra, pinto beans, fried chicken, blackberry cobbler. Fried chicken is one of my favorite food. I know fried chicken has stereotypical connotations for African Americans. I had long since made it known to my friends that I was not going to let any doggone ethnic stigma keep me from enjoying good fried chicken.

Through another door, Mr. Tobes took me to my room, the penthouse of Tobes Motel. He was very proud that I would be spending the night in it.

"You should be very comfortable here," he proudly said. "If you need anything, just let me know, all right?"

"Yes, sir."

We bid each other good night.

* * * * *

When I took a second look at the commode, I noticed that it hadn't flushed properly. As a matter of fact, it was overflowing in the penthouse!

How could this have happened? This is terribly embarrassing. The first black to ever stay in the penthouse in Tobes Motel and look what this dude has done! Unbelievable! How will I get out of this? And the Tobes have been nice and considerate.

I eventually got up enough nerves to call. I braced myself and dialed the phone.

"Mr. Tobes, this is Leo McGee," I mumbled, barely able to hear my own voice. "The commode doesn't work in my room."

"It doesn't?" he responded, sounding quite surprised.

"No, sir."

"I'll be right there."

Mr. Tobes proudly took care of the problem in about three minutes flat. I did not use the commode again during the entire quarter. Too risky!

On Monday morning, Charlie Golden met me at the front door of Henderson Hall. He was smiling from ear to ear. He began to rant even before we reached his office.

"Leo, I have gotten a very good report from those good people up in Oneida," he said. "You really wowed them. I knew you would. They think you hung the moon. I knew you weren't going to have any problems. People are just people everywhere you go. Leo, what's your secret?"

"What do you mean?" I asked.

"What did you do to wow those people that way?"

"Nothing in particular," I responded. "However, they were convinced that I was a spitting image of Bill Cosby."

Charlie sort of stared at me in disbelief. "By the way," he continued, "you really made an impression on the Tobeses. They are looking forward to having you back for the rest of the quarter."

For the remainder of the quarter, going to Oneida was the highlight of my week. I looked forward to having scrumptious meals with the Tobeses and sleeping in their penthouse. The desserts were unbelievable—peach cobbler, banana pudding, sock-it-to-me cake, pound cake, caramel cheese cake, chocolate cheese cake, coconut cake, pumpkin pie, blackberry cobbler.

The Tobeses' grandchildren elevated me to celebrity status in Oneida. Occasionally, I accompanied the whole family to the town's skating rink. There, I met family, friends, and children. I feel certain I was the very first black that a majority of the youngsters had ever seen in living color. Some asked for an autograph. It was difficult for me to convince them that I really didn't know Michael Jackson and Charlie Pride.

CROWBAR HAS TENURE

"President watching" is not a new phenomenon. It has existed since the appointment of the first college president. In its purest form, it is discovering how presidents behave on the job and elsewhere. Most of us within the academy and a number of those outside consider themselves experts in this pastime. Essentially, we engage in this exercise on a daily basis in an attempt to get a fixed perception of the campus CEO. The general expectation is that CEOs will stand tall in all situations in which they are confronted, no matter the level of contentiousness.

A colleague at Tennessee Tech, who is an active bird-watcher, informed me that "president watching" is a lot like bird-watching. In both cases, one is attempting to discover how subjects behave. He went on to say that certain bird behaviors have been documented in the literature. A few bird behaviors he mentioned included putting their head in the sand, excreting when excited, and bullying.

During my career as an academician, "president watching" became one of my favorite pastimes. The literature is replete with studies that identify qualities and characteristics of successful presidents. I preferred to focus on a short list that included temperament, relationships, sympathy and empathy, humor, and hobby.

- *Temperament.* An even temper is virtuous. When the temperament of others is pushed to the limit, the calm and collected usually are victorious.
- *Relationships.* Relationships are at the heart of presidential responsibilities and image building. Those who are able to establish and maintain effective relationships on and off campus will win many supporters.

- *Sympathy and empathy.* Effective leaders seem to have the ability to both sympathize and empathize with the work group.
- *Humor.* An appropriate sense of humor helps the president. Many are capable of using it to defuse contentious situations.
- *Hobby.* Having a hobby portrays the president as a real person. It also may provide constituents an avenue to identify with the president.

After several years of employment in Tennessee, I was satisfied that I had come across a president who embodied all of the qualities and characteristics that I valued most highly. He was Jack Norton, president of Ridgeview State Community College. Upon our acquaintance, we established a professional bond. He exuded extraordinary confidence, exceptional professionalism, and the persona of a seasoned higher-education stalwart. Conversing with him was always refreshing. Without fail, he elevated my self-esteem each time we met. I never passed up an opportunity to stop by his campus to visit with my new surrogate mentor. Moreover, we would seek each other out and chat at professional meetings. Simply put, Jack Norton was "top drawer, no dust."

On one of my visits to Ridgeview State Community College, a dog was sprawled on the doormat in front of the entrance to the administration building. He was a typical mutt. As I approached the door, he raised his head slightly, tail pouncing on the doormat. The moment I opened the door, he came alive and dashed into the building, turned the corner, and disappeared in a flash. I had no idea where he went. I became concerned. This was the first thing I mentioned to Dr. Norton when I entered his office.

He chuckled. "Ah, that's just ole Crowbar," he said, smiling heartily. "Why, ole Crowbar has been around here for several years, maybe six or seven I would guess. He's a regular member of the Ridgeview family. Indeed, he is. I bet Tennessee Tech doesn't have a diverse family like we have at Ridgeview, does it?"

I laughed. "I don't think so."

"You see, we are a lot more liberal at the community college level than you guys are at the university level," he teased. "We are a lot more family-oriented."

Both of us stood there giggling with his office door open. I wondered what the ladies out front thought of all this.

"Obviously, I haven't told you the full story about Crowbar, have I?" Dr. Norton asked.

"No," I replied.

"Then you must hear it," he offered. "Sit down, Dr. McGee, because this might take a while. You're not in a big hurry, are you?"

"No."

"Would you like some coffee," he asked.

"Coffee sounds great," I responded.

"Would you like anything in it?"

"Yes, two cubes of sugar."

"Sara!" he yelled.

"Yes, sir!" Sara answered.

"Would you bring two cups of coffee, one cup with two cubes of sugar."

"Yes, sir."

"Now, Leo, this is the story of our family member by the name of Crowbar. Somebody dropped Crowbar off on campus, let's say seven years ago. He was just a huge puppy. I could tell that he was a puppy because he wasn't quite filled out like a full-grown dog. The very first time we crossed paths, we became big buddies. He was just as friendly as could be but very undernourished. I thought I'd give him the name Crowbar because it just seemed to be fitting for him.

"I had some Graham crackers in the office, so I gave him some. And at lunch time, I went out and bought some dried dog food and gave that to him. The next morning when I came in to work around 7:30, he was at the front door waiting for me. I gave him his breakfast. We have continued this routine over all these years. Of course, the students feed him some during the day. They seem to like him quite a bit. He roams in and out of buildings at will. But really, he prefers to be outside.

"A few years ago, Crowbar caused a bit of a stir among some of our faculty. One of the junior faculty members thought it was high time that we got rid of Crowbar. He didn't think the Ridgeview campus was the proper place for a dog, let alone one having the freedom to roam freely on campus. He was pretty hot under the collar by the time he came to speak with me. I had gotten wind of this prior to his arrival. He wanted to lead me to believe that he had a pretty good faculty following. I sat very quietly and listened to him rant and rave for about fifteen minutes. I asked him had he finished. He said he had. Then I asked him if he had tenure (I already knew the answer). Of course, he said no. I politely told him that Crowbar has tenure, and he'll be here as long as he wants unless he commits a felony or something like that. I told him that I didn't believe Crowbar had it, in his gentle heart, to do something like that. Leo, to this day, I haven't heard another complaint about Crowbar. Not one.

"Crowbar is getting on up in years. He won't be with us much longer. It has really been a joy having him around. The students just love him."

DADDY, CAN THEY MAKE YOU GRADUATE?

In 1977, when my family moved to Cookeville, our daughters were eleven and four years of age. They had a great time growing up on the campus of Tennessee Tech. When they were ready for college, my wife and I acquiesced, letting them experience college life on a different campus—the University of Tennessee. Our youngest was more of a challenge while in college.

Jennifer, like Cassandra, was not permitted to take her car to Knoxville until the beginning of her sophomore year. She had kept her end of the deal. Her grades were quite impressive. In addition, she had made the cheerleading squad at one of the football powerhouses in America! Our baby was in second heaven!

I got this phone call at the office from Jennifer. She was hysterical, crying uncontrollably.

"What's the matter, Jennifer?" I calmly asked, bracing myself for the worse.

"Daddy, somebody broke the window out of my car and glass is all over the front seat!" she exclaimed.

"Was your car parked on campus?" I asked, rather pointedly.

"No. It was parked on one of the side streets," she responded.

"You might want to consider parking it on campus," I offered. "In fact, I would suggest that you park it as close to the campus police station as you can."

"I have to leave campus a lot, Daddy, and I can't ever find a place on campus!" she retorted. "It's impossible for me to always find a parking place near the police station on this campus! This campus is not at all like Tennessee Tech! It's much bigger, and there are a lot more cars on campus!"

Two weeks later, I got another phone call at the office from Jennifer.

"What is it this time, Jennifer?" I asked sternly.

Her disposition was the same as before. "Daddy, they won't leave my car alone!" she exclaimed.

"What happened?" I inquired.

"Daddy, they have been walking on my car!"

"Walking on your car?"

"Yeah, Daddy, walking on my car!"

"Jennifer, how do you know they've been walking on your car?"

"Because there are great big ole sneaker prints all over the top of the car, and the hood and the top are bent way in!"

"Was your car parked near the campus police station?"

There was silence.

From that point on, during my periodic meetings on the campus of the University of Tennessee or anywhere in East Tennessee, I would drive by the UT campus police station to see if Jennifer's car was in the vicinity. Without fail, it was always parked near the front door of the station. I couldn't help but chuckle.

It was two years before I received another call at the office from Jennifer.

She was not hysterical but emphatic. "Daddy, I just want to ask you a question," she said.

"What is your question?"

"Daddy, can they make you graduate?"

"Can they make you graduate?" I repeated. "Is that your question?"

"Yes."

"Jennifer, what kind of question is that?"

"I have another year to be a cheerleader, and I don't want to graduate. Peyton Manning is going to be the starting quarterback next season. There is going to be a lot of excitement on campus next year. Since I have completed all of the courses for my degree, my friends are telling me that the university is going to make me graduate, but I don't want to graduate. Can they make me?"

I chuckled but not loud enough for her to hear. "No, Jennifer, they can't make you graduate," I said. "Change your major and don't apply for graduation."

Before I finished, I could sense how excited she was. "Dad, thanks so much." she said.

EMPTY THOSE CHEERLEADERS' SATCHELS

The University of Tennessee cheerleaders joined the entourage on the chartered bus that was headed for Gator Country. The football teams would, no doubt, engage in a fierce battle in the swamp. As usual, a test of wit and wisdom between Fulmer and Spurrier would be the hallmark of this awaited and brutal endeavor!

Along the way, a stop was made in Chattanooga for a pep rally. During all of the excitement, somehow a bottle of fine wine found its way into to the hands of each cheerleader, a gift if you please! The recipients were overjoyed! However, they soon learned how pain can sometimes follow temporary euphoria. When they got back on the bus, to their chagrin, university officials confiscated their gifts, all fourteen bottles!

"Daddy, they made us so mad!" Jennifer exclaimed. "Those people in Chattanooga gave that wine to us, not to university administrators! Who are they to take our wine?"

"Jennifer, why did they take your wine?" I asked, trying not to chuckle as I already had a probable answer to my question.

"They just made up some stuff!" she said, obviously getting more agitated as she talked. "They said it was illegal for students to be given alcoholic beverages by boosters! Who do they think we are? We are not babies! We know how to drink responsibly. They said the university could get into big trouble if the administration ignored this. We didn't believe that stuff!"

"What did they do with all that wine?" I asked, chuckling under my breath.

"They kept it to drink for themselves, I guess. Since I am captain of the team, the other cheerleaders tried to get me to register a complaint with the president. I said, 'Ain't no way!'

"What would I look like going into the president's office and saying, 'Dr. Johnson, I would like to register a complaint.'

"And he would say, 'What's the matter, Jennifer?' And my response would be, 'Dr. Johnson, the athletics department took our wine.' No way!"

WAIT UNTIL TOMORROW

At the time Jennifer decided to continue at the undergraduate level for another year, I had no idea that her decision to stay another year was a premonition of what was to follow—four years of medical school and five years of residency. At her wedding rehearsal in 2003, she was still driving the 1984 car she took to Knoxville her sophomore year. At the rehearsal dinner, she sashayed up to me and said, "Daddy, my car stopped, and there is gas leaking. Do you think it will cost very much to get it fixed?"

I politely whispered in her ear, "Wait until tomorrow and ask your husband."

A NEAR SLIP OF
THE SCALPEL

After being around the athletics program at the University of Tennessee as a cheerleader for four years and after living in the big city of New Orleans for two more in surgical residency at Tulane, Jennifer had managed to obtain a personality transplant. It would be hard for most to believe that her formative years were spent in Cookeville, Tennessee.

Jennifer had an eight-week rotation at the hospital in Edgehill, Louisiana. She called one night to tell me about her experience with her first patient in Edgehill.

"Dad, he was a Cajun red-neck prisoner from the local jail. He was in to have his gallbladder removed. On the night before his surgery, I went to his room to introduce myself and explain what procedures were involved in the surgery. I walked into the room, held out my hand and said, 'Hi, Jim Ed. I'm Dr. McGee, and I'll be doing your surgery tomorrow.'

"Dad, that dude just stared at me. Then he said, 'Damn, I wish I hadn't let my insurance run out.'

"I said, 'I'm outta here, buddy.' Then I simply turned around and walked out."

The next morning, while Jim Ed was on the table being prepped for surgery, he was just lying there staring at Jennifer with that mean look on his face. They now had him strapped to the table, hooked up to the IV machine, and had a mask over his nose. They were about ready to put him to sleep.

Jennifer looked around to see if there was anyone other than Jim Ed paying attention to her. No one was. She took the meanest-looking scalpel from the tray and leaned down real close to Jim Ed and said, "Good buddy, when you wake up from this operation, you're going to be missing more than a damn gallbladder."

Jennifer said Jim Ed went into a panic mode and tried to get off the table. The head doctor ran over and said, "Hey, young man, lie still. You can't get up now." He then yelled to the anesthesiologist to put him to sleep.

Once the patient was asleep, the head doctor took Jennifer aside and asked what she had done to upset the patient so.

She said, "Dr. Margolis, last night when I went into his room to introduce myself, he said he didn't want no woman, especially no black woman, operating on him. So this morning, I tried to reassure him that his operation would go just fine and that he was in good hands with me."

Jennifer said when Jim Ed woke up from his surgery, the first thing he did was make sure the family jewels were still in place.

"Got you!" she said then winked at him.

Jennifer said when Jim Ed came back to the hospital for his post operation visit, he had a huge smile on his face. And he shook her hand.

He said, "Doc, my sister said you did a good job on my stitches. She said there ain't hardly no marks. I'm definitely gonna ask for you if I have to have my gallbladder removed again."

BREAKFAST FOR RESIDENTS

As I was preparing to leave the house for Kroger early one morning during the Christmas holidays, I asked Jennifer and my wife, Gloria, if there was anything I could bring back. Without hesitation, Jennifer said, "Yeah dad, bring me back a six pack of Guinness beer."

My wife nearly passed out! I stood there in total shock! I'm sure my mouth was wide open. In an attempt to calm us, Jennifer then said, "Mom and dad, the medical students at Tulane University always have beer and eggs for breakfast."

While in the beer section at Kroger, the thing I had feared most on the way to the store did happen. Who caught me frantically looking for the beer whose name I had now forgotten? He was the retired chair of the accounting department at Tennessee Tech.

I cleared my throat then mumbled, "I'm looking for a six-pack of Guinness beer for my daughter."

"I'm looking for a six-pack of Guinness beer for my daughter too, Leo," he responded while continuing to push his shopping cart down the aisle.

I didn't see a six-pack of Guinness beer, so I bought another brand. It was not acceptable to my daughter.

CHANCELLOR GEE, WE ARE DELIGHTED THAT YOU STOPPED BY AUGUST 2006

Gordon Gee is one of my favorite people and has been for many years. I became acquainted with him when he was maestro the first time ('90–'97) of that great midwestern university in Columbus, Ohio, that renamed itself in the 1970s—*the* Ohio State University. I can heckle a bit here without impunity because I received two- and one-half degrees from that institution. There will be no revelation regarding the half degree, however. From OSU, Gordon landed at Brown University then on to Vanderbilt.

Two years after his arrival, he initiated an activity with new faculty that has become a tradition. The August 17th visit by Gordon and his troop of forty-five new faculty members to the Tennessee Tech Appalachian Center for Craft is what prompted me to attempt to capture the essence of this noteworthy endeavor. This endeavor is dubbed the "road scholars" tour. Gordon, bow tie and all, boards a passenger bus along with the future of Vanderbilt and spends two days touring various spots in Tennessee.

"I want our new faculty to get a sense of what Tennessee is like," he said with pride.

This year, the tour went eastward from Nashville to Maryville and back with several stops in between. At the craft center, our visitors from Nashville were greeted by Robert Bell, president of Tennessee Tech, the director of the center, and me. Following this brief session, the group watched demonstrations in the glass and clay studios. After the demonstrations, it was time for some shopping in the center gallery. Wow, did they shop! We loved having the privileged contribute rather liberally to the state of Tennessee.

Gordon has a special way of intriguing his colleagues in higher education. As a leader in the higher education enterprise, he lives on the edge. He is bold, if you like. After spending over thirty years as an administrator, I have concluded that boldness is at the heart of educational transition. Gordon's relationship with the higher education community across this nation is, in some ways, likened to the now defunct TV commercial, "When E. F. Hutton speaks, everybody listens."

Many of us were stunned by Gordon's boldness when he advocated a revamping of the athletics industry in higher education. His advocacy for change in athletics was not simply mental gymnastics. He put his thoughts into action on his campus. Maybe his model is already experiencing a glimmer of success. After all, Jay Cutler is destined to be a star quarterback in the NFL (Denver)—the first from Vanderbilt since Bill Wade of the 1960s.

What can higher education across this nation learn from the "road scholars" tour? At face value, this experience is perhaps more powerful than I can adequately describe.

Bonding is the sine qua non—bonding among the newcomers and bonding between the newcomers and their chancellor. Perhaps the faculty can easily perceive their chancellor as a friend who is genuinely concerned about their success in the academy. What can be nobler? This innovative process of bonding will, no doubt, redound to the tremendous benefit of the institution for years to come. I sense that Gordon recognizes that each new faculty is a potential Nobel Prize winner. It is very likely that the "road scholars" tour will leave an indelible impression on the minds of the faculty. How could it not.

During Gordon's tenure as president of OSU the first time around, a small group of us were invited back to be recognized for outstanding achievements. There was an evening banquet and a breakfast with the president the next morning. I asked Gordon if he remembered me.

"I can't say that I do," he slowly responded then quickly added, "If you had been a big donor, I am sure I would have."

PROFESSOR, HAVE YOU BEEN BALING HAY?

On Monday around 3:00 a.m., I was awakened by excruciating pain in my chest. It felt as if my sternum was on fire. I waited for the pain to go down my left arm and to be followed by the clammy feeling. Fire ruled, however, lingering in my sternum! No place else!

I started to wake my wife then decided against it. She was sleeping too soundly. Plus, she would make a great big deal out of the situation—probably call an ambulance and wake the entire neighborhood! Neighbors would be turning on lights and rushing to front doors. How would one of the most devout salad-eaters and avid tennis players in Cookeville live down such an episode? I wasn't equipped to live through all the commotion!

So I quietly got up, struggled to dress myself and headed off to Cookeville General Hospital. Once I exited the neighborhood, excessive fear began to take control of my body. As I closed in on First Street and Dixie Avenue, I was sure I would be found right in front of Walter Derryberry's house, dead! I imagined some of the forthcoming cynicism would go something like this:

"I thought Leo had a PhD! Where did he get it from, Sears?"

"You mean professors at Tech are that stupid?"

"Why on earth didn't he wake his wife?"

"I guess stupidity can also be found in some crevices of the ivory tower too!"

"That guy was absolutely stupid!"

For some unknown reason, I thought about the times I cheated Peter Field and Derryl Martin in tennis. I suppose I wanted forgiveness before checking out. It was too late! My car literally went into automatic pilot and got me to the hospital parking lot. After stagger-ing into the emergency room, to the best of my ability, I said to the lady at the desk, "Ma'am, I believe I am having a heart attack."

She casually looked up and said, "What kind of insurance do you have?"

"Blue Cross." I whimpered.

She continued her casual approach to my painful problem. "On a scale of one to ten, in comparison to the worse pain you have ever had, how would you rate the pain you have now?" she asked.

"Eleven," I said, hoping to get her excited.

It worked! She then escorted me to another room and asked me to lie down on the table. She said she would get someone to come in to see me. A young man came in a few minutes later to do an EKG. He hooked me up, gathered the data, and left the room. Later an African American doctor came in with this long sheet of EKG data.

I smiled, feeling comforted to some degree, then said, "Hey brother, do you think I'm going to make it?"

He said, "Well, Professor McGee, you are not having a heart attack, and you have not had one. There is a gentleman down the hall who came in just before you with identical symptoms. The only difference is he was having a heart attack. He said he had been bal-ing hay all day. I don't know anything about baling hay. I am from Washington, D.C. Have you been baling hay?"

"No, sir," I responded.

It occurred to me that I needed to get out of this "brother" mentality with the doctor and get serious—find out the real skinny about this fire in my chest. It had not subsided in the least. Several times since arriving, I had felt really faint.

"Doc," I began to plead in the most pitiful manner I knew how, "since I have not had a heart attack and I am not having one, do you think I am going to have one?"

"Professor, I can't promise you anything," he responded rather sternly. "You might, or you might not have one."

"Should I go to Nashville to St. Thomas to have them check me out?"

"That's probably not a bad idea. Would you like for me to make arrangements, getting an ambulance and talking to the people at St. Thomas?"

"Yes, I would," I responded, feeling a sense of relief and pity at the same time.

The doctor came back to the room shortly and indicated that everything was arranged and that the ambulance was on its way. I suddenly realized that my wife, Gloria, was in the dark on all of this.

Once in the ambulance, my main expectation was quickly shattered. I expected limo type comfort. It was not to be! Between the siren and the exceptionally bumpy eighty-two-mile ride, my pain elevated by several octaves. The ambulance crew was most attentive, trying to ensure my survival and comfort the best they knew how.

When I arrived at St. Thomas, the cardiology team was waiting. As I lay on the table in the cold operating room, a lady came up to me with a clipboard.

"Mr. McGee," she said, "this may seem inappropriate at this time, but I must ask you two questions. Do you have a living will?"

Now I was sure the end was near. "Yes, ma'am," I said, although not knowing whether my will was living or dead. However, I was content giving her the answer she wanted.

"Do you have a power of attorney?"

I thought she had asked if I had a powerful attorney. "Yes, ma'am," I responded. "I have a powerful attorney."

I was awakened by the doctor who said rather emphatically that I had no blockages anywhere, not even in the aorta! I was disappointed because the pain in my chest was still excruciating.

I was taken to my room where I had to face my wife, Gloria, and my two daughters, Cassandra and Jennifer. I was hooked up to lots of stuff. This was my assessment: Gloria wanted to slap me. Cassandra was already grieving my death. Jennifer had already appointed herself head of the cardiology team at St. Thomas although her specialty is general surgery. The way the nurses started hopping and the doctors started eyeing her, I was sure I was in for a hard time. I was taken to other labs for further tests. All were negative.

When I was back in my room, confined to my bed by a heart monitor (among other things), eventually things settled down. My best of kin went out for a meal. I was all alone and, at this point, had figured out the source of my problem. *This is my chance*, I thought! I remembered that Gloria had placed my overnight kit in the bathroom. I gingerly but very quickly unhooked all my connections and made a dash to the bathroom and got my overnight kit before the nurse came rushing in. I took something out of my kit and consumed it; and within fifteen minutes, my pain was completely gone.

The commercial for this story is "if all else fails, chew a Rolaids. Just one of those little tablets could save you $12,000. Remember, Rolaids! It's spelled R-O-L-A-I-D-S!"

EPILOGUE

Growing up on a truck patch (mini farm) in Arkansas, I observed firsthand how Negroes eked out a living with their meager resources. They place a high priority on canning fruits and vegetables, preserving meat, hunting, and fishing. Trees loaded with fruit were highly-valued, prized resources! These trees taunted the hungry stomachs of the young. I unscrupulously got my share of this forbidden fruit, peaches in particular. In this process of easing the hunger in my stomach, I learned to eat peaches before they were ripe. I dared not take a chance for them to ripen because the point they did, the women in the community would confiscate them for canning. Therefore, as a youngster, I learned to eat peaches before they were fully ripened (green). I only like them that way now, no soft, mushy peach for me!

Now the skinny, the day before my "fire in the chest" episode, I had worked in my office from early morning to early evening. I was working on an accreditation report (Southern Association of Colleges and Schools—SACS). When I realized I hadn't eaten lunch, I headed to the grocery store to purchase some fruit. Guess what, the green peaches were staring at me. They were huge! I mean huge, huge, the largest I had ever seen. I bought two. Back at the office, I consumed both of them. Fifteen minutes later, I had a stomach ache. It finally waned, and I forgot all about my acidic snack until my condition had baffled both Cookeville General and St. Thomas hospitals.

"Skunkology" in the Curriculum

A troop of crafty skunks took refuge under the heating unit at the McGee's home. I headed to the farmers' co-op for help.

"Professor, all you need is a trap," the gentleman behind the counter advised confidently.

"What kind of bait should I put in the trap?" I asked.

"Any kind of vegetables," he responded. "Those damn things will eat nearly anything, cat food, dog food, hot dogs, sardines, fruit, anything. They ain't that particular at all."

"What will I do with the skunk after I trap it?" I queried.

"Shoot it!" he exclaimed.

I was aghast, knowing that it was probably illegal to shoot within the city limits. Yet I left the co-op with a $40 animal trap. With vegetables inside, I placed the trap near the patio wall. A week passed, no skunk.

I sensed that I needed to get academic about the matter. I went to the internet. I found this article: "Skunks! A question of common 'scents.' Bait trap with hotdog."

Two days later my wife, Gloria, called me from home to give me the good news.

"There's a skunk in the trap," she said excitedly. "It's really fat."

I gasped. "I'll be there soon," I responded, not really knowing what I was going to do with a trapped skunk. But surely an associate vice president for academic affairs would be able to figure something out. After all, skunks, better known as polecats, were a part of the fabric back in rural Arkansas. Our dogs were always getting sprayed. Actually, my brother and I got sprayed once during our preteen years.

We were chasing two polecats in an open field. Because one was only able to get a portion of its body into a hole, the back half was in perfect position to cast a hefty spray. Got yah! My mother insisted that both of us sleep in the corn crib for a number of nights.

When my wife heard the car pull in the driveway, she positioned herself in the window for a ringside view. As I slowly walked toward the trap, shielding myself with the patio wall, I heard this little bitty pitiful "meow." It was our own black cat, Ebony.

Two cats later and on a Saturday morning around seven o'clock, I discovered that I had indeed finally trapped a real skunk. Our plane for New Orleans was scheduled to leave at eleven o'clock.

Gloria rushed and called the animal patrol number. She was informed that the animal patrol people only work Monday through Friday and was told that the police department sometimes helps out on weekends.

A police officer arrived twenty minutes later. This is the gist of the conversation between the officer and Professor Gloria McGee. I listened from another room.

"Ma'am," the officer said, appearing concerned but not really, "I understand that y'all have trapped a skunk?"

"Yes, we have," Professor McGee responded with anticipation.

"Is it one of the city's traps, or is it y'all's personal trap?"

"It's a personal trap." Wrong answer!

"Well, I can't do anything. We're not allowed to touch a personal trap."

"Officer," Professor McGee now pleading, "we are going to be out of town for the rest of the weekend. What are we going to do with this skunk?"

"Turn it loose," he said with finality.

"You mean you want us to turn it loose after all the trouble we've gone through to catch it?"

"Yes, ma'am."

"We don't want to do that."

"Well, you can feed it," he offered.

"Feed it?" Professor McGee queried angrily.

"Yes, ma'am."

"That doesn't make any sense."

"I am so sorry, ma'am. There isn't anything I can do. Y'all will just have to wait for the animal patrol guy to come on Monday morning. He should be here the first thing on Monday morning. I will make sure that this will be his first stop."

The animal patrol guy arrived on Monday morning around 7:15. He was whistling as he trekked around back, appearing to be happy to take care of this small order of his daily routine. I was sure this was going to be the highlight of my twenty-six years in Cookeville, Cookeville's animal patrol czar in action mind you!

I watched with excitement as the czar began to ready himself for this mammoth task.

"Sir, how long have you been in this business?" I asked.

"Twenty-two years," he replied with pride.

"Have you ever been sprayed by a skunk?"

"Never," he quickly responded. "Not a single time," he boasted.

"You mean you've never been sprayed in twenty-two years?" I probed.

"Nope."

"That's remarkable."

"You just have to know what you are doing. I've been in the business a long time."

"How are you going to get that skunk without it spraying?" I continued to query.

"Just watch," he offered, exhibiting utmost confidence. "I am going to gently put a cover over the cage and pick it up."

I was getting more excited by the seconds.

He continued, "It's no problem. Just stand back and watch. Generally, skunks will cooperate if you are really gentle with them."

Just as the czar began to gently work his magic with the plastic cover, he accidentally kicked the cage. That little skunk turned into a fire truck. Now there was quite an ebb and flow of expletives coming from the czar of twenty-two years.

I knew but asked anyway, "Did it spray you?"

There was no response, but there were a few more choice expletives.

"Did he spray you?" I asked again.

"You damn straight!" he blurted. "You got me out rhythm by asking so many questions."

I wanted to get the most from this clinic. I continued, "How many more times can it spray?"

"On and on, I reckon," he offered more gently.

ESOTERICALLY SPEAKING

Articulation agreement! What's that? During the early 1990s, state universities in Tennessee initiated an aggressive process of developing articulation agreements with public community colleges. This was to ensure that students moving from community colleges would have a seamless transfer to the system's senior institutions. Although many laypersons had difficulty understanding this esoteric higher education jargon, they yielded to the intellect of those who had the upper hand in this endeavor—the high and mighty academicians.

In this regard, Tennessee Tech's goal was to develop articulation agreements with eight community colleges. To get the process started, President Angelo Volpe, Associate Vice President Rebecca Tolbert, and I crisscrossed the region to open up lines of communication between leaders at Tech and their counterparts at the community colleges. By leaving as early as 5:00 a.m. on some mornings, it took us about three weeks to complete this task. We tried to make the trips as interesting as possible. We ate at the finest restaurant in Harriman, namely Captain D's. We went across the ferry near Cleveland. We thought about stopping at Jack Daniels distillery over near Tullahoma, but our better judgment kicked in.

As the Tennessee Tech team was leaving Tullahoma one February afternoon, an official car with blue flashing lights pulled up behind us. I was driving. My days in Chicago flashed through my mind. I stopped the car and immediately got out and went back to the car with the blue flashing lights. With my hand held out, I said, "Good afternoon, officer. I am Bill Cosby, and I am doubling as a chauffeur today." The officer was literally speechless. Before he could say anything, I continued, "I was the black history speaker at Motlow State Community College today."

The officer was still speechless. He struggled to clear his throat. When it appeared that he had succeeded, he began to speak, "That Frank Glass is a nice president at the college, isn't he?"

"Yes, sir," I agreed with enthusiasm. "He's one of the best."

"He sure is." He paused. "Y'all be careful, you hear."

"Yes, sir."

Within minutes, we were on our way again. Becky and Angelo were impressed. I could tell. Curiosity got the best of Angelo.

"Leo, how did you talk him out of a ticket?" he asked.

"I told him I was Bill Cosby and that you two were NBC executives and that we were filming in the area."

PROFESSOR IN THE CORN PATCH

In addition to serenity and ease of traffic flow, colleges located in small communities tend to have many other advantages. Institutions' employees and the general public promulgated these perceived positive aspects whenever an opportunity presents itself—nice place to raise a family, low crime rate, etc. In addition to these benefits, during the summer months, institutions' employees shared garden produce on a regular basis—tomatoes, squash, okra, corn, peppers, etc.

Corn is my favorite vegetable. Most of the gardeners at Tennessee Tech knew this. Throughout my thirty-year career at the university, my coworkers kept me supplied with numerous varieties of sweet and field corn. What a tremendous delight for me but not for my wife, however. She abhorred the messes I made as I attempted to prepare the corn for consumption.

One of my colleagues in the college of engineering grew an extra-large garden. He planted a vast majority of his garden in field corn, Hickory King to be exact. This variety of corn is generally fed to animals. However, I would drool from the time he planted this variety in the spring until the time it was ready to eat in late summer. My colleague was thoroughly convinced that from the time Hickory King was ready to be plucked, there was about a thirty-six-hour time frame to get the corn off the stalk. If this task was not completed in due time, the corn would be too hard for human consumption. Therefore, in late August, I anxiously awaited Sid Gilbreath's phone call.

I shall never forget the follow-up phone call I got from him after I plucked corn from his garden in 2007.

After Sid identified himself, it took him a while to stop laughing. When the laughing began to subside, he said, "Sorry, Leo." He burst into a hefty laugh again. "Sorry," he managed to say. He continued, "Leo, I got a phone call from a neighbor the other day." I could tell that he was straining to keep from bursting into a laugh again. "I thought pretty hard about my neighbor's call before I made the decision to call you. You are a pretty good sport, so I made the decisions to share the conversation I had with my neighbor. Are you ready?"

"Yes, I guess," I said hesitantly.

"You have to understand my neighbor. She's getting on up in age. Plus, she's from the very old school. Do you kind of get my drift?"

"I guess," I responded. I had my ear pressed to the phone but wasn't sure I wanted to hear the punch line.

"Are you still there?" he asked, still chuckling.

"Yeah, I'm here, Sid."

"No offense, okay?"

"No offense."

"When Mrs. Bryant called, she was nearly out of breath. I couldn't figure out what was going on. I thought maybe her husband had fallen, or he had had a heart attack. She said, 'Sid, there was a colored man stealing corn from your corn patch in the broad daylight.' I died laughing when she said that. I let her continue. 'He was dressed in a suit and tie, and he got two great big ole bags of corn. Sid, why are you laughing so much?'

"'Because that black man is a vice president at Tennessee Tech, and he's a good friend of mine.'

"'He is? I thought it was kind of strange for him to be stealing somebody's corn in the broad daylight. But you never know what people might do these days. Nowadays, folks'll do just about anything. Thanks for straightening me out, Sid. I was just trying to be a good neighbor as usual.'

"'I know, Mrs. Bryant. If you see any stranger people in my garden, be sure to let me know. Okay?'"

MURDER BY MEMO

Memorandum

To: Dr. Leo McGee
                   Associate Vice President for Academic Affairs

From: Jack Taylor
                   Professor of Animal Husbandry

Subject: Rumor

Date: March 9, 1996

Over the past two or three days I have heard from several sources a rumor to the effect that beginning next academic year, all grades must be reported using voice mail.

- I am sick and tired of people telling me that I must attend sessions to learn to do something that I do not want to do anyway;
- I am sick and tired of "innovations" which make things easier for some clerk or administrator but significantly increase the burden on me;
- I absolutely refuse to have anything to do with voice mail. Not now! Not tomorrow! Not ever!

KNOWING WHEN THE DEAL IS DONE

"Paul, you have done a great job of maintaining your weight over the years," commented Jeff, a colleague of Professor Paul Stuckey of the history department. "What is your secret?"

"It all starts with a good breakfast," Paul responded.

"What do you have for breakfast?"

"I have cold cereal. It's always Raisin Bran."

"I love Raisin Bran. Why do you have Raisin Bran?"

"Because it's really a well-balanced meal. I probably fix mine a bit differently than other people."

"What do you mean?" Jeff inquired.

"I buy the raisins and the bran separately, and then I mix them."

"Why do you do it that way?"

"It's cheaper."

REVERED DEAN

For two years at Philander Smith College, I had observed a really old gentleman ambling around campus. He could be seen all times of day and infrequently at night. Occasionally, he could be seen talking with faculty members. Mostly, he was to himself, simply ambling around campus with a perpetual smile on his face. When he would go behind the serving line in the cafeteria to serve himself, no one seemed to pay any attention to him. I was a bit puzzled by it all and so were others. Eventually I learned that he had been some sort of dean at the college. My football buddies and I didn't have any idea what a dean was. It was just a word to us, although we figured it must have been a very important position.

The president's office was located on the second floor of the fine arts building, which also housed the campus library. There was a long sidewalk that stretched past the president's office and ended at the entrance of the library. Because this long sidewalk led to the library, it was not traversed very frequently by football players.

On this sunny spring day, several of us football players were standing around on this long sidewalk shooting the breeze. We were, of course, quite a distance from the entrance to the library.

Without notice, I felt a gentle tap on my shoulder. I looked around; and to my surprise, it was this really old gentleman that ambled around campus all the time. He was staring at me with that perpetual smile. I stared back at him and smiled but not knowing what to say or what to do.

He slowly opened his mouth, and this is what came out. "Young man, do you know where I live?"

"No, sir," I responded, quite puzzled.

"I don't either," he said rather emphatically.

We continued to stare at each other. The president's secretary, Mrs. Woods, must have been looking out the second-floor window and observed the exchange and my puzzled expression.

"McGee!" She yelled, "Tell Dr. Martin to stand right there and that you'll be right back. Would you come up to the president's office for a minute?"

"Yes, ma'am," I responded then passed her order to Dr. Martin.

Mrs. Woods met me in the hallway. "What did Dr. Martin want?" she demanded.

"He said he didn't know where he lived," I responded.

"Lord, have mercy," she said. "We are really worried about him. This is the second time this week he couldn't find his way home. He's going downhill really fast. He lives at 1203 Izard. Would you be kind enough to take him home?"

"Yes, ma'am."

"He never locks his doors. That worries us too. The president would really appreciate it if you took him home. He loves Dr. Martin with all his heart, but he should have retired long ago. You don't mind taking him home, do you?"

"No, ma'am, I would be glad to."

"Thanks so much, McGee. I'll probably have to call on you again. Is that okay?"

"Yes, ma'am."

In no time at all, Dr. Martin and I became the best of friends. During several of my visits to his home, I had noticed lids from different sized jars lined up around the kitchen wall with food in them.

"Why are those lids lined up around the wall?" I asked.

"They are for my friends," he gleefully responded.

"Friends?" I asked, puzzled.

"Yes, they are my international friends," he responded, obviously being evasive.

I didn't press the issue. I simply took him at his word although I was taken aback by this secrecy. Perhaps I had made too much of our friendship. I must admit, however, that I thought openness from him was warranted.

Now Dr. Martin would find me on campus and simply stand a few feet away and wait for me to extend an invitation to take him home. On most occasions, I would be shooting the breeze with the guys or would be in the company of my girlfriend, Gloria. I shall never forget this one occasion when I accompanied him home. As usual, his front door was unlocked. Once inside, he plopped down on the sofa. I walked down the hall and noticed from a distance that the kitchen door was ajar. Suddenly, I found myself petrified. I had never seen animals like these. What on earth—

"Dr. Martin!" I screamed. "There are some things in here on the kitchen floor!"

"Those are my international friends," he said calmly. "When they get really hungry, they come inside for a snack."

"What are they?" I asked.

"They are horned lizards from Guatemala. My kids had several when they were young. Somehow, they got out of the cage and began to reproduce outside. I leave the backdoor open for them to come inside when they want a snack."

Is This Your Car?

I had my first serious encounter with the concept of retirement while I was employed at one of three universities, which shall remain nameless. I observed through my office window an elderly friend who was walking around in the parking lot as if he was having trouble finding his car. Thirty minutes later, as I was leaving the campus for home that afternoon, he was still looking for his car.

I drove to where my friend was now standing. He looked as if he was pondering his next move. I let down my window. Charlie looked completely exhausted.

I stared at him. He stared back at me. "Charlie, what on earth are you doing?" I asked jokingly.

"I can't find my damn car, man," Charlie responded. Frustration and embarrassment were written all over his person.

I wanted to laugh but steeled myself. "What kind of car do you have?" I asked.

"I just bought myself a new Toyota Camry," he responded.

"What color is it?"

"Beige," he answered.

"Man, you have been out here a long time," I teased. "I've been watching you from my office window for at least thirty minutes."

"You have?"

"I sure have," I said and braced myself for Charlie's response. I could tell that he was getting a tad agitated.

"Is that all you high-level administrators have to do is look out your windows and watch people in the parking lot?"

"No, Charlie," I quipped. "It was the way you were out here walking around in circles that caught my attention."

"I just don't understand it, Leo. I know I parked in this lot this morning, but my car is nowhere to be found."

"You think somebody stole it?"

"Beats me. I've never heard of a car being stolen from our parking lots, have you?"

"No, but there can always be a first time. Are you sure you parked in this lot?"

"I am positive," he responded with all the resolve he could muster. I always park in Duncan Hall parking lot."

"Why don't you get in my car, and we'll drive around and see if we can find your car."

"Sounds like a winner to me," he gladly said, looking tremendously relieved. When he flopped into the seat of my car, he took a deep breath.

As we drove around with the window down, Charlie took his remote key and literally clicked on every Toyota in Duncan Hall parking lot. Nothing happened! We circled the entire parking lot once more. Charlie clicked incessantly. Again, nothing happened!

"Charlie, are you sure that remote works?" I asked.

"Yes, Leo, it works," he responded, again sounding a bit agitated. "It's brand new, man. It always works."

After all of that useless cruising around in the parking lot, I had begun to wonder whether or not Charlie's wife had driven him to work that day. Plus the tennis match I had scheduled that afternoon was weighing heavily on my mind, but I didn't want to leave my friend.

"Charlie, why don't I try the Baxter Hall parking lot," I offered.

"There is no need to," he said emphatically. "I always park in Duncan Hall parking lot."

"Why don't I try it anyway," I insisted.

"You can try it if you like, but it won't do any good. I never park way over there," he assured me.

As we circled the Baxter Hall parking lot, I spotted only one beige car. I pulled up behind it.

"Charlie, there is a beige car," I said.

"Not the right beige, Leo," he quickly said. "What make is the car anyway?"

"It's a Nissan Altima," I responded.

"Wrong make, wrong color," he said with great resolve. "The only car I ever drive is a Toyota Camry. I've been driving Toyota Camrys for the past thirty years."

"Charlie, just click on the car," I demanded.

"Okay, Leo, I'll do it just to satisfy you and show you that you're barking up the wrong tree."

The instant he clicked, lights began to flash all over the car. He then turned to me and said, "Those damn engineering students have pulled another prank on me."

PERCEPTUAL TENDENCIES

An alumnus of Franklin Methodist University, who was a Methodist by faith, approached the president of the university to inquire about having the campus chaplain perform a funeral service for his recently deceased dog. The president responded by saying, "I can't bring myself to ask the campus chaplain to do something like that. He only conducts funeral services for humans."

The alumnus went on to say, "Fritzie has been in our family for over thirteen years. And my wife, Lucy, and I just can't stand the thought of burying her without some type of funeral. You would please us very much, Mr. President, if you would agree to have your chaplain perform this special favor for us."

The president very politely and very kindly refused the alum again.

The alum then said, "In our will, Lucy and I plan to donate $5 million to the university, but I guess we will have to find someone else to conduct a funeral service for our Fritzie.

The president then said, "Why didn't you tell me Fritzie was a Methodist?"

WORDS FOR THE FAINTHEARTED

Bits and pieces of the following clichés have been in circulation in the higher-education arena for many years. The attempt here is to make them more meaningful to the reader. No pretense is made herein to suggest that originality is in the forefront.

- *Picking fights.* If you see an Internal Revenue Service official fighting a bear, help the bear.
- *Wallet.* Beware if you see a sign in the window or a department store that reads "we are here to please if it takes every penny you got."
- *Pet.* Be suspicious if you see a sign on a place of business that reads "veterinarian/taxidermist, either way you get your dog back."
- *Career ladder.* If you are not the lead dog, the scenery never changes.
- *Assertiveness.* You have got to be forthright enough to advise your colleague to get out of the saddle when his horse is dead.
- *Workplace uncertainty.* Beware that whatever hits the fan will not be distributed equally.
- *Favorite cocktail.* Never take a drink from a urologist.
- *Workplace decorum.* When you get frustrated and you must tell someone where to go, try to help that person look forward to the trip.

- *Leadership style.* Avoid using the "seagull" leadership style. That is, a leader who flies in, makes a lot of noise, messes all over the place, and then leaves.
- *Dog days of an administrator.* As an administrator, beware that some days you are going to feel like a milk bucket under a bull.
- *Personnel change.* If your cow will not give milk, sell him.
- *Collegiality in the workplace.* Beware that lions can indeed lie down with lambs, but lambs will not get much sleep.
- *Extrapolation.* Think in terms of creative extrapolation if you see an advertisement on a plumber's truck that reads "a good flush beats a full house."
- *Baldness.* God made a limited number of perfect heads; then he made some with hair. God gave us a certain number of hormones. It's shameful that some bodies wasted them on hair.
- *Happiness.* If you want happiness for an hour, take a nap. If you want happiness for a day, go fishing. And if you want happiness for a month, get married.
- *Intuitiveness.* If you find yourself in a hole, the first thing you must do is stop digging.
- *Work habits.* If your boss catches you sleeping at your desk, what you should do is say, "In Jesus's name I pray. Amen."
- *Professorate.* People who like to dominate conversations and who always have to be right usually die young. Scientists call these people professors.
- *Retirement.* When you reach retirement age, retire while you can still recognize your car.

Refined humor and a genuine smile can often be more effective than the flamboyance we occasionally bring to the table. These resources in tandem are grossly undervalued and grossly underutilized in the academy.

MY RETIREMENT

One afternoon around 4:45, during the spring semester of 2007, I found myself having difficulty finding my car in the Henderson Hall parking lot. After ten minutes of searching, I concluded that someone had stolen my car. I phoned the campus police.

"Are you absolutely sure you parked in this parking lot?" the officer asked.

"I'm absolutely sure," I responded rather emphatically. "I always park in Henderson Hall parking lot!"

The campus officer radioed the city police department. After writing down the specifics, the city officer offered to drive me home. While in the car, I remembered a TTU colleague who had retired the next morning after having had difficulty finding his car in a campus parking lot.

On this particular afternoon, my wife, Gloria, happened to be looking out the window when the police car drove up. When I entered the house, she was clearly in panic mode.

"Leo why are you coming home in a police car?" she demanded.

"Someone stole my car from the Henderson Hall parking lot!" I responded. "Right from a parking lot on the campus of Tennessee Tech, mind you!" I ranted. "Can you believe that?"

Gloria's surprised expression confused me. "Honey, your car hasn't been stolen," she calmly admonished. "It's being serviced. I drove you to work this morning. Remember?"

The next morning, I submitted my retirement letter!

About the Author

Leo McGee entered college in 1959 as a student athlete. Football was his sport of choice. He began his professional career as a public-school teacher in Chicago and Columbus, Ohio. After three years on the job, Ohio State University beckoned him to do a graduate study. There he earned the master's and PhD degrees. The institution summoned him to be assistant director and director of clinical experience in the college of education. Then there was the position of curriculum chair at Tennessee State University. His OSU mentor, now president of Tennessee Technological University, insisted that he join him.

During his thirty-year career at TTU, McGee was assistant dean, associate dean, assistant VP, associate VP, and interim VP for academic affairs. He has written or cowritten five books on subjects relating to African American studies, grant acquisition for classroom teachers, and regional Tennessee history. His current title is associate vice president and professor emeritus.

CPSIA information can be obtained
at www.ICGtesting.com
Printed in the USA
LVHW110019170919
631287LV00001B/25/P